D1078319

DRIVING
THE GREEN

An Irish Golfing Adventure

Kevin Markham started playing golf at the age of six and has played ever since. After ten years' working in London and Dublin, he became a freelance copywriter and took the opportunity to lay a lot more golf. Not for the better it turns out. He writes about golf for newspapers, magazines and blogs. His first book was *Hooked – An Amateur's Guide to the Golf Courses of Ireland* (2011).

Kevin has an active online presence through his blog and social media. He also has over 7,000 golf course photographs on his Flickr page.

www.theirishgolfblog.com
www.flickr.com/photos/kevinmarkham
www.twitter.com/kevinmarkham
www.facebook.com/HookedOnIrishGolf

DRIVING THE GREEN

An Irish Golfing Adventure

KEVIN MARKHAM

The Collins Press

FIRST PUBLISHED IN 2014 BY
The Collins Press
West Link Park
Doughcloyne
Wilton
Cork

© Kevin Markham 2014

A CIP record for this book is available from the British Library.

Paperback ISBN: 9781848891982
PDF eBook ISBN: 9781848898448
EPUB eBook ISBN: 9781848898455
Kindle ISBN: 9781848898462

Typesetting by Patricia Hope, Dublin
Typeset in Sabon
Printed in Malta by Gutenberg Press Limited

This book is dedicated to greenkeepers everywhere – the men and women who slave over our courses, making our fairways play so beautifully and our greens run like silk. You are rarely seen and rarely given the respect you deserve for working in all kinds of weather so that we golfers can enjoy our game.

On my travels you appeared with breakfast (Raymond at Killymoon), located errant balls, retrieved golf clubs and took time to have a chat. Thank you . . . although that does not extend to the greenkeeper who cost me my first hole-in-one!

CONTENTS

Pat on the Back

'I've got a feeling for the game of golf. I did very well on the course in Skegness, until I got stuck in one of the little wooden windmills.'

Rɪɢsʙʏ, *Rising Damp*

Orange wellington boots. Not the obvious choice of footwear on a golf course, but I was only eight years old and Barley Cove's nine-hole course was a minefield of cowpats. It was fortunate that my fashion imperatives and practical sensibilities combined so seamlessly. Over the years I have committed many crimes against fashion, but in those boots I rocked.

I had been playing golf for a few years, taught by my father and grandfather. Their hallowed golfing ground was Greystones Golf Club, but it wasn't somewhere an eight-year-old boy could get to easily. Barley Cove in County Cork, however, was a regular family summer destination and it had a links golf course right on the doorstep. On these summer holidays we would hire a chalet overlooking the beach and holes that stretched across the dunes. Most days I played it twice, getting up at the crack of dawn and sneaking out. On the first occasions when I disappeared into that early morning mist, my mother arose to find her son gone, probably kidnapped. My dad was booted out of bed to find me. And when he did, somehow he'd managed to bring his clubs too.

Every morning, at that ridiculous hour, I would head off in my wellies with Granddad's cut-down clubs, some old balls and the wild seaside air in my soul. The course was about as natural a creation as you could find. Fairways ran an obvious route between distinct dunes, with a tee at one end and a green at the other. It really was as simple as that. Barley Cove was crammed with the usual links hazards but the cowpats were extra special. Cows have little understanding of golf etiquette. Fairways, rough, tee boxes – wherever a golf ball could go, you could be sure that a cow had already left its calling card. Except the greens. A holiday course it might have been, but even here the greens were sacred. They were enclosed by electric wire fencing and the cows never went near them. The wire ran all the way around the green at a height of about two feet. There was a gate that golfers would open and close, but sometimes when you were on the opposite side of the green you simply stepped over it. Two feet. It doesn't sound very high but for an eight-year-old boy, whose crotch happened to be at the exact same height as the electric wire, it was a severe obstacle.

I have always been told that you learn from your mistakes. The mistake I made that day, as my most sensitive parts made contact with a current strong enough to repel a 1,000-lb animal, has left me with a deep appreciation of the power and pain of electricity.

In 1998, married and in my thirties, I returned from eight years in London, and finally got back to golf. I played occasionally in the UK but it is almost impossible to get a regular game unless you are a member somewhere.

I fell in love with the game again and wanted to play as many courses as possible. Naturally, the big-name courses held most appeal but playing all of them was an unrealistic dream.

'Has anyone heard of Newcastle West?' Ronan asked as we sat in the Greystones clubhouse one day.

Three of us shook our heads, so the following Monday I went to Dublin's Hodges Figgis bookshop and searched in the sports section for Newcastle West. There was next to nothing. The only reference I found was to a 'pleasant parkland with big trees'. Greystones Golf Club was similarly dismissed with a one-line description.

That was wrong.

I started to have ideas for a golf book of my own – a book that would review every Irish eighteen-hole golf course equally, from an amateur's perspective. It wouldn't dwell on history or the designer; it wouldn't pander to a course because of its reputation; and it would be about the golf experience, pure and simple.

The question was, how could I play every course without losing my house and, quite possibly, my wife? I mapped out potential routes and calculated how many golf clubs I'd have to visit. The number started at 326 (the official Golfing Union of Ireland figure), but I found another 23 along the way – some as I was passing the gates.

There was also the matter of how much this was going to cost. If I stayed at B&Bs or hotels and ate out in clubhouses every day, it was going to cost in the region of €15,000. It was not a figure I could justify and reality stamped on my enthusiasm.

'Get a camper van,' my wife suggested. 'You can always sell it afterwards.'

I returned to the maps, back on plan. Now I had to figure out how best to approach golf clubs to ask them if I could play their course. The main goal was not to pay a green fee. Yes, I know this sounds cheap, but consider the alternative: if you work on an average green fee of €50, multiply that by 349, you end up with over €17,000. I decided the easiest thing to do would be to seek the advice of Royal County Down, a world-famous club with two links courses. I phoned up and asked what I should do. The voice at the other end of the phone said, 'You'll need to contact either the Northern Irish Tourist Board or Tourism Ireland and ask them to write to us on your behalf, requesting a round of golf and when you would like to play. We will contact them with our response and they will then contact you. In order to acknowledge our generosity you must bring your first born to be sacrificed to the golfing gods of the north.'

I asked the obvious question: 'Is this to play both courses or just the Championship one?'

Some courses were always going to be difficult to access: I had already played Royal County Down, Royal Portrush and The K Club, but I expected Old Head, Ballybunion, Lahinch, Doonbeg and Portmarnock to be problematic. As it turned out, only one of these proved awkward. In general, getting to play Ireland's courses was an easy exercise. Perhaps that reflects the generous nature of Irish people and the way that fellow golfers are embraced on this island. I made a phone call, explained what I was doing and the manager, secretary, or professional went out of their way to accommodate me. A few requested an email to clarify things, but I was keeping a blog and I had a publisher behind me, which was usually more than enough to satisfy anyone who reckoned I was pulling a fast one. And those who still thought I was after a freebie only had to look at my camper van to realise that if that was the case, I was one sad and lonely individual.

With the camper van confirmed as my preferred mode of transport, I set about buying one. It was something I knew nothing about. A friend of the family offered to help, so I listed out my requirements and budget. A jack-of-all-trades, he had fingers in plenty of pies and eventually said he'd found the perfect vehicle in Athlone. A week or so later he turns up in this 1989 Hymer. It was big, wide and top heavy. I was assured the engine was running fine and that everything was in working order. He showed me how to use the old-style gear stick, the fridge, the water system, the gas hob, the toilet, the shower, the gas tank . . . the list went on, but as soon as he showed me I promptly forgot.

It was also left-hand drive.

Unfortunately, not everything worked quite as efficiently as I had been led to believe.

I had problems with my gas. The heater and hob worked fine, but the gas-powered refrigerator was a different story. It was the most complex piece of equipment I had ever encountered. True, there were only two controls, one of which was an on/off switch, but the temperature dial had to be pressed in and turned until the flame caught – a sound so faint you'd have had a better chance hearing a fart in a storm. When travelling it was recommended that I turn the gas off, which meant that I had to turn it back on when parked. This was an operation that saw me down on my knees every night, ear pressed against the fridge door as I turned the dial one millimetre at a time. It could take seconds or minutes depending on what was going on in the outside world. Either way, the job was only half done because I then had to select the temperature. It appeared there were only two settings on the dial: 'warm' and 'frozen'. I lost count of the number of times I had to throw out curdled milk. I also lost count of the number of times I ended up with a frozen milk carton. I never did get it right and, after a couple of months, gave up trying.

The gas aside, the water supply, which came from a large container under one of the seats, also had to be figured out. It was rigged to supply the loo, shower and kitchen sink, although not in that order, I hasten to add. There was little to no pressure and the shower had barely enough power to wash a small rodent. By the time the hot water had come out of the showerhead and reached the tray it was cold. I ended up using the space for storage. I never regretted my decision, apart from the time at Greenore Golf Club, when I stepped out of their shower and gave the lady cleaner a bigger surprise than she might have expected at that hour of the morning.

The problem, however, was the water-pressure system itself. If I wanted water from the kitchen tap, I could get it only by going into the bathroom and turning on the tap in the sink first. I had to leave it running while I used the kitchen tap and then turn it off afterwards. And hot water was an impossibility.

I didn't see why I should keep all of these idiosyncrasies to myself. 'Come for a ride,' I said to my wife one day. 'I need to fill up with diesel.'

She came. She saw. She never stepped foot in it again, which was only mildly ironic since it had been her idea. There went my plans for cheap future holidays.

In fairness, I understood why. Being a man, I'm not exactly fastidious when it comes to cleanliness and I hadn't done any tidying in the camper van. My wife had been reluctant to touch anything.

The wall-to-wall shagpile carpet was an unexpected flourish. At the start, I thought it was grey, but underneath the filth it was red. It was the bright orange and brown multi-patterned curtains, however, that made me nauseous. I went on a 1970s' acid trip every time I closed them. I'm not sure what it all said about the previous owner, but I doubt he had to do drugs when he just had to look at the fabric. Or sniff it for that matter.

It was a strange feeling having your bedroom, dining room, kitchen, sitting room and bathroom in one tiny space. You couldn't swing a cat in it, yet alone a 9 iron. And this was a four-person camper van, supposedly. If one other person had been in there for a week I would have killed him. Or her. So it was just as well that my wife had been so dismissive.

The bed was a pull-down double. It hugged the ceiling above the driver's and passenger's seats, and then pulled down about three feet when it was required. You had to clamber up and down a bit, balancing on one of the sofas (where, incidentally, someone's head would be if there were four people on board).

Over the course of my journeys I grew to love the old banger. It was a temperamental piece of junk, but it had a certain *je ne sais quoi*. To drive it was to drive a boat. It rocked from side to side, leaned into corners like a comb-over on a windy day and didn't much like the idea of braking. In terms of speed . . . not a lot.

The biggest challenge in my new mode of transport was the Irish roads. The joy of our roads can only be appreciated if you have had the pleasure of experiencing them first-hand. To try to describe them to the uninitiated would be to do them a severe injustice. Country roads can be like an airplane during violent turbulence . . . no two parts of your body go in the same direction. Oh sure, the county council lads come out and fill in the potholes, but it's like putting a plaster on a gaping wound. No sooner have they poured in the tar and the gravel than the rain comes and washes it all out again. Still, it keeps them in employment, I suppose. They can come back to the same spot and do exactly the same thing up to three or four times a year. Even Pavlov's dogs would have realised that this was a pointless battle, but the councils insist on banging away with the same tired methods. Of course, that assumes you're lucky enough to live in a county where the potholes get filled in. A man by the name of Martin Hannigan, in County Cavan, took huge exception to the lack of council efforts to fill in potholes, and started driving around the county painting yellow circles around offending craters. His mission was ended in 2009, when a judge told him to desist or face jail. The man should have been given a medal or, at the very least, a shovel and some tar. No one seemed to spot the irony that, at the end of one of the worst roads in the county, there was a new roundabout bedecked with freshly planted flowerbeds and young, staked trees.

The problem in the camper van, given its size, was that a pothole sent the vehicle into a sort of freeze-frame orbit. Anything that wasn't tied down ended up floating in space until touchdown, at which point everything crashed to the floor, usually a long way from where it started. My quest may have focused on Irish golf, but I drove around enough of Ireland to know that I could have written an opus on Irish roads as well.

The other challenge was drivers on the road. No one wants to get stuck behind a lumbering, fat beast of a camper van but how drivers dealt with my presence demonstrated a dangerously devil-may-care approach.

One of my best friends, a sales rep at the time, once told me that the worst drivers in Ireland were from Tipperary South.

'And the second worst?' I asked.

'Tipperary North.'

Perhaps a bit harsh, but I encountered some nutters on my travels, many of them young men who felt that being in what amounts to a small tin can meant they could not be harmed. Overtaking on corners, ignoring traffic lights, and this crazy assumption that drivers coming in the opposite direction would automatically move onto the hard shoulder if they started to overtake. My camper never went much above 90 km/h and I could see these guys going mental if I was a fraction under the speed limit. They would weave from side to side, head pressed against the glass or out the window to see past my ample rear. Then, inexplicably, they would make their move. I'd watch in horror as a Jenson Button-wannabe roared past, scattering the oncoming traffic like a dog chasing seagulls on the beach . . . except a dog has more intelligence.

When I passed through Charleville on my initial golfing foray into Cork, I spotted a car parked by the side of the road. You couldn't miss it. The car vibrated and twitched to the booming music that was trying to escape through heavily tinted windows. It was white, with fancy headlights, funky alloys and a spoiler that screamed 'have I got a hot rod in my pants or am I just pleased to see you?' This wasn't the first such vehicle I had encountered – boy racers are not limited to specific Irish counties: they're equally as macho and stupid wherever you go – but it was the first disco-in-a-car I had come across. Under the chassis, lights flashed in time to the music. Everyone who walked past the car stared at it in disbelief and then moved on, glancing back over their shoulder to check if it was real. And all that time the little boys inside would be revelling in how hard and cool they were. It would work too, once their balls dropped.

I've always been amused by boy (and girl) racers. I guess they start with a budget and then sit around identifying all those crucial 'boy racer' essentials: 18-inch alloys and extra-wide wheels – check; tinted windows – check; spoiler – check; super-fat exhaust – check; bucket seats, 7,000 megawatt stereo, furry dice – check . . . and after they've budgeted for all of these items they suddenly realise they have all the cool stuff but no car. With only €250 left, off they go and create their super-charged, extra-funky, 10,000-brake horsepower Nissan Micra. Yeah man, that's cool.

I thought about adding some furry dice to the camper van, but gave up on the idea. Besides, I had James Last to listen to and nothing's cooler than that!

A Rusty Start

'If you think it's difficult to meet new people, try picking up the wrong golf ball.'

JACK LEMMON

'Where will you be on Judgement Day?'

The question caught me off guard. I glanced across at the young woman in the passenger seat. Dark brown hair framed her face and rested on her shoulders. She was attractive, lithe and in her thirties. She was also serious. I wanted to point out that this was my camper van, so my rules, which meant no religious stuff before 9 a.m. I became acutely aware that her husband was sitting somewhere behind me, out of sight.

It was my first trip, going through Waterford, Tipperary and Cork, and I'd been apprehensive when I left home at 6 a.m. I'd planned thoroughly, but something about taking that first big step jangled my nerves. Less than an hour later I'd seen this couple hitching outside New Ross. I decided to do the Christian thing and, with luck, calm my nerves at the same time. Brenda was Australian, John was British, and they'd been married for five years. After a bit of chit-chat about my travels in Oz and their travels here, Brenda launched into stories about their holiday in China. That's when the hairs on the back of my neck started to rise.

'Then John broke his leg,' she said in a hushed tone.

'Sorry to hear that,' I said, searching in the rear view mirror for the elusive John. 'How did that happen?'

'He fell,' she said sharply as if it was obvious, or irrelevant, or both. 'But the villagers who rescued us cured him. Within two weeks he could walk over red hot coals.'

I laughed, assuming it was a laughing moment. It wasn't.

'It was a miracle.' Brenda's voice had become evangelical and I still hadn't found John in the mirror. I wanted to know why a man who had broken his leg would then choose to walk over hot coals. Was it verrucas?

As I watched the roadside fly by, all hedgerows and soft green fields, I wondered how I had managed to pick up a couple of crazies on my first trip. The camper van was left-hand drive so those grassy fields were within reach . . . if I timed the jump just right.

'Where will you be on Judgement Day?' she repeated, clearly annoyed that I had drifted off at this critical juncture.

'I hadn't given it much thought,' I capitulated, having decided that 'Watching *EastEnders*' was not a prudent response. For all I knew, they were *Coronation Street* fans.

She drew herself up and stared with steely green eyes that threatened to pop out of her head. 'I,' she proclaimed, 'will be sitting at God's right hand.'

Phew, I thought, definitely Corrie fans.

'And I will be judging you.'

My, someone had a mighty high opinion of herself.

Of course, Brenda and John weren't crazy. They were born-again Christians. Their Chinese experiences had converted them from normal people into raving loonies. For the next forty-five minutes I heard how I too could be saved if I allowed myself to be born again.

I wondered fleetingly if they should be thrown from the moving vehicle rather than myself. Would they be born again if they hit the ground at 80 kilometres an hour?

I crossed the wide swathe of the River Suir and entered Waterford city, desperate to be rid of my passengers. As they alighted, John followed meekly behind his wife. He hadn't said a word since Brenda's ravings began. I had no idea what he had been doing behind me. Performing some religious ceremony perhaps, or maybe he was secretly delighted that the fervour of Brenda's devotion had been directed at someone else for a while. She was still pleading with me to join them on their journey as I drowned them in a cloud of camper-van exhaust.

A short time later I crossed more water, the Kings Channel, on the ferry that serves the Waterford Castle Golf Club. It covers an island that is the exclusive domain of the golf club and the Waterford Castle Hotel alongside. I was standing on the 1st tee in sunshine, the dew shimmering on the fairway which stretched towards the distant waters. This was the first hole on the first course of my golfing quest. I tried to get excited, to tell myself that this was the start of something special, something I had been dreaming about for years. But Brenda's religious fervour had messed me up. I pretended it was her head I was teeing up, but as I started my downswing out popped a pair of demented eyes.

My duffed drive didn't even reach the ladies' tee box.

'Bollocks.'

I rattled around Waterford city's golf courses, before arriving late at Dunmore East. It's a small fishing village and the chipper was doing a roaring trade as I drove past. It started to rain as I headed up the hill, the harbour to my right. *Golf. Rain.* Two words that most Irish golfers tie into a sentence one week after another. In the clubhouse I ordered some grub and a pint and sat by the window enjoying the sound of the rain against the glass. As I was to discover in many clubhouses, when you pull out a laptop people are drawn to you like a magnet, which is how I spent my first evening in the company of Mick and Dermot. Mick was a big man with a smile that rippled from ear to ear. He was a summer visitor from Dublin and played regularly at Dunmore East, when the family came down. Dermot seemed content to watch proceedings with his pint hovering inches from his mouth, always looking like he was about to say something but never quite getting there. After I'd explained what I was doing I fielded the questions that became part and parcel of many clubhouse nights and rounds of golf.

'What's your favourite course? How did you manage to get a job like this? Has your wife divorced you yet?'

As my dinner arrived, the lads excused themselves, leaving me to write up my reviews before heading back for my first night's sleep.

You know that sound that infiltrates your dreams? The one that stays out of reach but keeps nipping at you until eventually it drags you out of your slumber? I opened my eyes in the dark and listened. It sounded like dripping . . . and it was coming from inside the camper van.

I sat bolt upright.

I discovered two things that night: the first was that I slept exceptionally well in a camper van; the second was that the ceiling was only a foot above my head.

My head ricocheted off the roof with a resounding crack that suggested I'd either broken the ceiling or split my forehead.

With my brain screaming and my mouth uttering obscenities, I switched on the light and searched for blood. The hole in the ceiling suggested I'd won that particular battle, but the angry bruise across my forehead darkened and spread for the next fortnight.

The rain and the dripping lasted till morning and the bowl placed underneath the leak only served to magnify the sound. Worse was to come as I discovered over the coming days that the rain would form a mini lake between the ceiling and roof. It happily sloshed around as I drove, mimicking the sound of the ocean washing over pebbles on the beach . . . very calming when you buy it on a CD but cause for concern when it flows overhead, about to leak through in an alarming number of places. I learned that I had to park at a particular angle if the leak was to be in the centre of the camper van, where I could lay out an assortment of bowls and containers to catch the water. I also learned that after a week of sunshine not all the water had gone. It had simply been hiding. At least the area above my bed stayed dry.

From Tramore to Dungarvan I followed a stretch of coastline known as the Copper Coast, for its copper mining heritage. It led me on to Youghal, the most easterly town in County Cork, where I encountered a bunch of Ladybirds on the back nine of Youghal Golf Club. Not wildlife but enthusiastic lady golfers who played every Monday, staying close to the clubhouse. I had interrupted their normal order of play, and while the first two groups happily invited me to play through, the third group, a two-ball, had other ideas.

'You can play through if you want, or you can join us.'

It was the 16th hole, a par three that stared out at Cabin Point across the Blackwater Estuary. The town of Youghal lay below, almost in hiding which seemed apt given the town's recent troubles. Once renowned for its manufacturing and carpet making, the town faded somewhat as its large factories closed over the past decade. It left a scar of unemployment and Youghal has endured the emigration of young people at a faster rate than elsewhere.

I joined the ladies, and Moira and Juliet let me tee off first before moving to their tee. Moira was a small, older lady who moved slowly and deliberately. Her silver hair flipped back and forth in the wind and she took what looked like an uncomfortable swing at the ball. It flew a little and then bounded straight down the hill towards the green.

'It's my hips,' she said by way of an apology. 'I've just had them replaced and this is my first game back. I'm a bit slow.'

Juliet's drive followed Moira's and we parted ways as I headed right to look for my errant ball. I glanced back to see how Moira was doing. I thought of my gran. There was something about her size, her hair, the way she moved that reminded me of my father's mum. And my gran played golf too.

We met on the green and Moira rolled in a 20-foot putt for par. The smile on her face lit up the course. She walked over to me, stood on tiptoe and planted a kiss on my cheek.

'Thank you,' she said, grinning at my embarrassment. 'That's only my third par ever.'

Moira's par and my use as a good luck charm were recounted in detail back in the clubhouse when the twelve Ladybirds swarmed around me.

'Where are you playing next?' Mary asked after my lunch arrived.

'East Cork,' I replied.

'Are you playing Water Rock?' She leaned over and stole a chip.

'Never heard of it. Does it have eighteen holes?'

'Oh yes. It's a family run place. Pay and play, you know. Very nice too.' The other ladies agreed. They told me how to find it and we chatted for a bit longer before they trooped off en masse.

I was enjoying the quiet clubhouse atmosphere when a voice in my ear made me jump.

'How did you stand it?' asked the voice.

'Stand what?' I replied, turning to find an elderly man stooping over me.

'Playing with women,' he said sharply. His face was flushed as red as his jumper.

'I've no problems playing with women,' I replied. 'Do you?'

He growled at me. 'Can't play golf so what's the point? Hold everybody up, don't they!'

An old friend of mine would disagree. Playing off 8, hitting the ball long and dead straight, Clare would beat most men I know. If you can swing a club, hit a ball and you want to play golf then you're as entitled to step on to a golf course as anyone else . . . and I'm happy to play with you. I played with a wide and entertaining group of golfers on my travels; fortunately this old fart wasn't one of them.

'Oh, I see. And I take it you've never held anybody up?'

'Humph.' He glared at me when he realised he wasn't going to get the reaction he wanted. I took that as my cue to leave.

The N25 road led me to Cork, Ireland's second city. There are twelve courses to choose from, both within the city and around the periphery, but there was one on this trip that particularly fascinated me. Blarney Golf Resort had opened only recently and it was designed by John 'Grip it and rip it' Daly (along with the considerable expertise of Irish golf architect Mel Flanagan). The resort came with a hotel, a spa and the ubiquitous rows of houses that gather around the hotel and clubhouse like the drool on a greedy property developer's gob.

Blarney is, of course, famous for something else: the beloved tradition of kissing the Blarney Stone. Tourists get fleeced for a few quid to be hung upside down so that they can kiss a piece of stone set in the walls of Blarney Castle. I take my hat off to the fella who had that idea. Does he get royalties? The stone was fitted into the castle's walls in the fifteenth century and has been busily kissed by thousands, if not millions, of people since then.

On my way through Blarney town I dropped off a load of my clothes at a laundrette. As I handed over the bag I was told to come back later the next day. Playing ten rounds of golf a week required certain things to be done: one was keeping the camper van from smelling like a fish factory, which meant clothes being cleaned; the other was trying to stay healthy.

I'm not exactly the fittest or most flexible golfer ever invented, so I had decided early on that to reduce the risk of injury, I would have a massage once a week. It would keep the stiffness out of my back, neck and shoulders – three areas that can ruin a golfer's game.

After a sun-kissed round at Blarney Golf Club, I headed for the hotel. Perhaps the words 'Beauty Spa' should have served as a warning. To most men, a spa is a place where women go for a few hours, to chat, gossip and gripe. Few men are sure what actually happens there and fewer are prepared to ask. Which is pretty much how most women feel about golf.

I was apprehensive as I approached the doors and this was compounded by the cloud of incense that greeted me as I entered. In the background, some kind of Far Eastern, Feng Shui music combo thing was going on and I felt a bit of a lemon when the two lady customers sitting in the reception gave me a rather disdainful once over. At least I'd changed out of my golf shoes.

The girls who worked there all wore black silk jackets emblazoned with the resort's red logo. I gave my name and was given a clipboard in return. I was directed to a chair where I was to fill in a form about my health and the treatment I wanted.

I ticked the box for 'Deep Massage' and 'Back and Shoulders' and returned the form. Then along came Polly, a diminutive dark-haired girl who looked at me like she'd drawn the short straw. She led me away to a treatment room that was so dark I almost stumbled over the massage table. Whales and dolphins were now singing love songs to each other, the Feng Shui musicians presumably crushed by the new arrivals. More incense filled the air. What is it with that stuff anyway? It makes me want to sneeze.

I stripped to my boxers, lay face down on the table and waited for a vigorous massage that never came. No, Polly's fingers poked and prodded at me like I was a piece of fruit and she was trying to decide if the Best Before date had expired.

And then she was done. I was told I could relax and sleep to help the treatment penetrate, but the whales had started their Westlife cover versions and I made a quick escape. By the time I left the spa and the hotel, the only thing that felt penetrated was my wallet.

Back in Blarney, one drive through the small town tells you that the economy survives on tourism. Colourful guesthouses and B&Bs make up the outskirts, which is why a laundrette must do very nicely.

'Hang on there, my love,' the same woman called from the back when I walked through the door. 'I'm almost done.'

I could see her sorting through my clothes. She was a heavy-set woman in a loose blue dress and sandals. With the clouds of steam billowing around her I understood her clothing choices, as well as the rosy cheeks I had encountered the previous day. She folded my shirts and t-shirts meticulously, then the trousers and then my jocks. Clearly she was talented at her craft but I found it disturbing watching her work. As a man, I only expect to see my mother folding my underpants.

She was as friendly as can be and tucked my clothes neatly into the bag I had given her. 'What happened to your head?' she asked, looking at my bruise.

'Kissing the Blarney Stone,' I replied.

From Blarney, wearing a clean shirt and a pristine pair of underpants, I followed the R618 west to Macroom, along the course of the River Lee. Macroom Golf Club is hidden away under an archway in the centre of the small town. Blink and you miss it, but it also takes a degree of conviction to believe that it's the entrance to a golf club. There are few golfers who expect an archway complete with towers, castellations and canons. This was the entrance to Macroom Castle which was burned to the ground in 1922. The demesne was purchased by locals in 1924 for the purpose of building a golf course. And a tasty little one it is too.

There was a Juniors competition ahead of me, some twenty boys and girls striding through the sunshine, and emitting laughter you rarely hear in the adult game. The jollity continued back in the clubhouse, with chicken and chips all round and a passion for Blackcurrant and soda.

I sat in the corner and listened to the brief speech given by the organiser of the day's competition. He batted away the friendly jibes from his audience until the big moment came and the room fell silent. The prizes started from sixth place and, as each winner stepped forward, there was a polite round of applause. Everything was going smoothly until they got to the overall winner. As the runner-up returned to his seat, a man hustled into the room from behind the bar and grabbed the organiser. Hushed words followed as they huddled together, peering covertly at the papers the second man had with him. It was like the Oscars, and the kids were getting restless.

The man in charge nodded furiously, shrugged and then nodded some more. Then he turned back to his audience.

'Ah,' he began.

That wasn't a good sign.

'I'm sorry to say we'll have to start all over again. A score card was missed.' He looked slightly glum and embarrassed at this turn of events, but after some groans of exasperation the five winners stood up and returned their prizes.

The golfer with the missed card came second and fair dues to the organiser who recovered his composure and awarded seven prizes instead of six.

Can you imagine the uproar if such a thing happened on Captain's Day? There'd be a lynching.

I was in the heart of Cork, Ireland's largest county. Renowned for its artisan foods, it is also home to three of Ireland's most popular cheesemakers: Charleville, Kanturk and Mitchelstown – all towns that I'd be visiting in the coming days.

I drove north, around the western edges of the Boggeragh

Mountains towards Kanturk, along narrow roads with valley views and the hues of clouds that splashed the landscape with colour. I drove past a half-built bungalow, a cow standing inside with its head resting in the space where a window should be. It looked thoroughly content as it gazed out at the world. I saw plenty of such bungalows, in the most unlikely places, but this was the only one I saw that was cow-friendly. Cheese must have been more important to the economy than I'd thought.

Later that day I stepped onto the tarmac at Charleville Golf Club. A golfer approached, pulling his trolley with that despondent air of a man who'd recently been defeated by an arduous round. When he saw me he perked up.

'Are you the fella walking around Ireland, carrying your clubs and playing all the links courses?' he asked.

I was standing next to a camper van at a parkland course some 40 miles from the sea. My clubs were sitting on a battered trolley.

Yes, I thought, an easy mistake to make. Instead, I smiled. 'No, that's Tom Coyne you're thinking of.'

A Philadelphian by the name of Tom Coyne had taken it upon himself to walk around Ireland's coastline, carrying his golf clubs and playing every links course on the island. He had a regular column in the *Irish Examiner* newspaper, which was a Corkman's newspaper of choice. This was neither the first nor the last time I was mistaken for Tom during my travels in the Rebel County.

'What are you doing then?'

'Playing every eighteen-hole course on the island,' I replied proudly.

He nodded, unimpressed. 'Good luck with that.' He was short, rotund and in his forties, so pretty much a mirror image of myself. Except he had hair. He wandered around the camper van, looking it up and down. 'Grand job. I'm Tony, by the way. What do you call her?'

'Who?' I enquired.

'The camper van. What do you call her?'

A few choice words came to mind. 'Nothing. I don't call her anything.'

He looked surprised. 'Really! I call mine Bessie. Yes, beautiful Bessie. She's a grand old girl but not as old as this one.' He stroked the front of the camper van like it was a beloved pet. I started feeling possessive.

'And what does your wife think of you calling your camper Bessie?'

'She doesn't mind. Not at all. Sure, she's Bessie, too. Avoids any confusion.'

What kind of confusion he was referring to, I didn't know. In the throes of passion when he called out Bessie's name, was he thinking of his wife or the camper van? Avoiding that kind of confusion I could understand.

I've always thought there were some strange folk in Cork.

Tony asked if he could step inside and I followed him in, pondering potential names.

When I had first explored the camper van – like a kid with a new toy – I discovered that I had a serious problem. This went far beyond the leaking roof, the fridge that converted food into icebergs and the shower that didn't work. No this was properly serious. The radio/tape deck didn't work. So no music from the latest, talentless boy band, no local ads for PJ's Curry House or Murphy's Showers, no sparkling wit from DJs so old they should be put back in the crypt, and no chat shows with angry callers complaining that the local newspaper hadn't provided detailed instructions on how to use the new zebra crossing. I was bereft.

Oh, sure, the tape deck worked, but that was part of the problem because there was a tape wedged inside. *James Last Plays ABBA's Greatest Hits*. ABBA, set to orchestral arrangements. I can think of worse ways to die, but not many. But it got worse: this was *James Last Plays ABBA's Greatest Hits ... Volume 1*. The mere thought that a Volume 2 existed gave me sleepless nights. What if it was lurking somewhere in the shagpile?

I used a knife, a skewer, foul language and my patented thump-kick-and-slam technique to try to remove the tape. Nothing worked. During my more lucid moments I wondered if the previous owner had done this deliberately. Did he want me to die of a cerebral haemorrhage or sell the camper back to him at a knock-down price? I finally succumbed and used a screwdriver to dig it out. I was past caring about the tape deck as long as the radio worked. Out it popped mid-'Take A Chance On Me'. After all that, I felt a certain affinity to an old music medium that had seen me through my teenage years. James Last never made it into my neatly-filed stacks of cassette boxes, but I decided the tape was part of the camper's history. It therefore deserved a place on the camper's dashboard, which is where Tony found it.

'Hey, we have the same taste in music,' he said, pulling the tape out of its box. 'This is one of my favourites.'

I had to beat him over the head to stop him putting it back in the deck.

After Bessie's husband/owner had departed I sat on the camper van step to change my shoes. My foot slipped and some rust flaked off. I looked at it lying on the tarmac. 'OK then, Rusty it is.'

Pat Nagle, Charleville's general manager, is a wiry man, with a wirier mop of dark hair. He gave me one of those crushing handshakes that you tend to reserve for matchplay opponents and led me towards the bar. He pointed out a scorecard above the door.

'Tiger Woods and Payne Stewart at Waterville,' he said. 'You're playing early tomorrow aren't you? Well, chances are you'll bump into Geoff. Ask him about the card.'

I stepped onto the 1st tee at 6.45 a.m., well behind someone who'd pulled into the car park half an hour before.

Charleville is a charming, tight, tree-lined course. There are so many trees I didn't see the golfer in front of me for some time, not until I caught him on the 9th. With the birds barely awake and most sane golfers still in bed, we agreed to hook up.

'Kevin,' I said, introducing myself.

'Geoff,' he responded.

I smiled and said that Pat had mentioned I might bump into him.

'I like playing early. I'm not really into playing competitions. I prefer to get out and knock it about, you know.'

Geoff was an Englishman and I asked how he came to be living in Cork.

A rather wistful look crossed his face. 'About fifteen years back, my wife and I had a holiday booked to Poland. At the last minute, the travel agent phoned up and said the holiday had been cancelled. She asked if we wanted our money back. I said no, we want to go on holiday. Where else can we go that's not too hot?'

He took a short, compact swing at the ball.

'"Ireland", she said to me. I'd never thought of coming to Ireland until then, and when we came over we fell in love with the place and decided to stay.'

We were on the 14th when I got around to asking him about the scorecard in the clubhouse.

'Oh,' he said, mildly embarrassed. 'That's mine. I donated it to the club after I joined.

'Tiger and Payne Stewart were playing in Waterville before the British Open, years back, and a good crowd turned up to watch them play, me included. They played a two-ball, better ball format and ripped the course to pieces. The length of some of Tiger's drives was phenomenal. And Payne Stewart's not exactly short off the tee.

'Anyway, I was marking a card and they went around in fourteen under. It was amazing to watch and, at the end, as they were walking back to the clubhouse I asked them to sign the card. Tiger wasn't interested but Payne couldn't have been a nicer gent.'

Donating the card to the club was a generous gesture, but I suppose what's the point of having something like that and locking it up in a drawer!

Our conversations continued all the way to the bar before Geoff asked if I'd like to pop back to his for lunch. As tempted as I was, I had to decline: I had a hurling final to go to.

I was heading to the village of Churchtown, a few miles from Charleville, where the North Cork Junior 'A' Hurling Championship Final was throwing in at two o'clock. It was the small village team from Ballyclough taking on Mallow town. I had played with the team's coach/manager, and one of their star players the day before at Kanturk: Kevin and Mark were there to release the tension of being in their first ever final.

Kevin was a big, sturdy Cork man with a belly chiselled in the Murphy's brewery. He hit a solid ball with powerful shoulders and was never too bothered where he ended up. Of the two, he was the more relaxed and, during our round, he invited me along to the match.

'You won't see a game like it. David and Goliath, this one. Mallow have been here before but they have no idea what we're capable of. We're ready for them.'

So, on the day of the final, I parked and strolled along the village streets in the company of dozens of people all heading in the same direction.

I had only been to hurling matches in Croke Park, where I was up in the stands and away from the action. Standing on the sidelines was a different matter entirely as I got to appreciate the speed of the game, while a few hundred screaming supporters created an atmosphere that flooded the ground. The match was frantic, going end to end, but definitely in favour of Mallow who were scoring freely. There was a growing unease among the Ballyclough fans. It was looking like a whitewash but it took only a second to turn things around.

One of Ballyclough's players broke clear, sidestepped and surged forward. The crowd surged with him, the voices rising to screams as the sliotar sailed between the posts. It was a piece of individual brilliance and moments later he was doing it again. The team responded and Mallow were left wrong-footed time and again as the smaller players used their agility and speed to outplay them. The points ticked over, the gap closed and the crowd sensed something magical was happening. Individual names were called out, impassioned support aimed at friends and loved ones, and it was utterly electrifying as the minutes counted down.

There was one point in it with a minute to go and the momentum was all Ballyclough's . . . but that was where it ended. A Mallow lad caught the sliotar and went on a rampage up the pitch, knocking opponents out of the way like Hulk Hogan through the tulips. He heaved his hurley and scored the vital point that reduced Ballyclough's fans to silence while Mallow's faithful went into raptures.

I watched the bowed heads of the Ballyclough players as they left the pitch. Kevin was offering encouragement but he looked devastated himself. So close and yet so far. It was heartbreaking and tense, and when I looked down the programme in my hand was completely crushed.

After the brutal rains at Dunmore East, I had enjoyed fine weather – the kind you don't notice until it's gone – and the day after the hurling I managed fifty-four holes, playing Mallow, Fermoy and Mitchelstown. The day delivered a panorama of views, from the Galty to the Knockmealdown Mountains, as well as delivering a panorama of aches and pains that stretched from my neck to my feet. It felt like sand behind my eyelids as I sat in the Mitchelstown clubhouse, trying to type and think at the same time. The pint was a bad idea, the alcohol hitting a system that was running on empty. I didn't quite appreciate how exhausted I was until one of the members sat down opposite me.

He had lots of questions. I had answers, but my brain had no intention of engaging with my mouth. The sounds that came out were unintelligible, but at least I didn't drool.

The man glanced at my pint, wondering no doubt how many I'd had.

The weather remained perfect over the following days, but I still managed to get soaked at Ballykisteen. The golf course is part of a hotel in County Tipperary, on the edge of the busy N24.

I felt the sun on my back as I walked to the pro shop, passing between the hotel's flower beds and bedrooms, and the back of the 9th green. Moments later I was walking back the other way, dripping wet. The two men I passed stared at the trail of water behind me, looked up at the cloudless blue sky and then back at me.

'Wait till they turn the sprinkler off on the 9th green,' I growled. 'It's spraying more of the hotel than the green.'

Fair dues to them: they didn't laugh.

It turned out they were my playing partners. John and Fergal worked for Iarnród Éireann and were in their fifties. They were both talkers. They were also golfers of the less cultured variety . . . they talked as I played shots, didn't repair pitch marks and didn't worry too much about trolley wheels rolling over greens. It wasn't long after starting that I realised they were also intent on digging a new Iarnród Éireann route, such was the furrow of unreplaced divots.

We had reached the 18th, a par five that aimed straight at the hotel, and the train track behind us was almost complete. Fergal buried his drive in the rough a few yards off the tee.

'I think I'll be leaving that where it is,' he said, reloading and knocking his second down the fairway. When we reached the ball he pulled out his trusty rescue club and hit an absolute stinger. The ball stayed no more than a foot off the ground as it rocketed towards the green. Up ahead, a crow was intently digging up the fairway. He never saw the ball that killed him. A squawk, an explosion of feathers and the crow collapsed.

Not a word was spoken as we approached. We stood over it, looking down at its lifeless eyes.

'Should we say a few words?' John asked, poking the bird with his shoe.

'Oh I have a few words all right,' said Fergal with annoyance. 'I'd have got another 50 yards at least.'

The camper van and I were never quite as one. As fond of Rusty as I became, the relationship was one-sided and strained from the very start. I expected some sort of bond to form but Rusty was unwilling to comply. I don't blame it. After all the abuse I inflicted I wouldn't like me either. I reversed into banks, buildings and bushes. I hit one bank so hard I practically tore off the rear bumper. And it's not like I was confined to tight spaces. No, on arriving at Gort Golf Club, in Galway, I was faced with an empty car park, so I decided to reverse up to the building and reversed into it instead. I ended up replacing the driver's side wing mirror three times. The awning, attached to the top of one side (and never used), had an unpleasant and losing encounter with a telegraph pole in Cahersiveen. There was barely one trip when I wasn't subjecting the camper to some level of abuse and I started as I meant to go on.

After Ballykisteen, I made for Dundrum on the R661. I crossed the Multeen River and arrived at some roadworks. A mobile traffic lights, no more than a yellow box with a stalk of lights above it, shone red. I was glad for it. Ahead of me, traffic cones squeezed my side of the road, creating a narrow strip of tarmac between the cones and the hedgerow. On the other side of the cones, workmen were struggling away in a long pit. There wasn't a lot of room and I felt myself gripping the steering wheel more tightly as the lights finally turned green.

I should have known there was something wrong as soon as I started. A loud scraping was followed by the mobile lights shifting a couple of feet. I was still trying to figure out what had happened when I clattered the first cone. It spun off into the pit, followed by the second and third. I was as close to the hedge as I could be, but the cones continued to perform like synchronised swimmers, tipping into the pit on top of the workmen as I sailed by. There were shouts of anger but it was too late to stop now. As I approached the end, I saw that one of the workmen had climbed out and was waving at me furiously. The last cone spun into the hole at his feet as I waved back and pressed down on the accelerator. A mile or so up the road I pulled in to assess the damage. There was none, but I discovered I'd left the side doorstep down, and it was this that had been colliding with the cones. I pulled the step up and never made that mistake again.

Despite the disappointing spa treatment at Blarney, my second attempt at a massage came a week later. My travels had taken me from Blarney, through County Cork and up into Tipperary, where I arrived at Dundrum House Hotel and Golf Resort, a few miles west of the heritage town of Cashel and its rock of the same name. I turned down a driveway that led between the trees to a Georgian manor house, sitting above the Multeen River. As a luxury country house hotel it offered all the comforts that Rusty did not.

I'd booked a massage with Jonjo, a sports masseuse who couldn't have been more different to Polly. He was of average build, but there were muscles bulging under the sleeves of his shirt and he looked like a man ready to work.

'What do you need?' he asked, as we stood in a small room in the basement of the hotel.

I explained what I was doing and how much golf I was playing.

'Are you having any problems at the moment?' He directed me to the table.

'My right shoulder is catching,' I replied.

He nodded. 'OK. Strip to your boxers and we'll get started.'

No incense. No whales. No mucking about.

Jonjo leaned in and his fingers dug deep. The only sound was the creaking of the table as he worked. He pulled my arm out to the side and pressed down on the shoulder blade. Things cracked and popped.

'Does it hurt if I do this?' he asked, rotating my arm.

I only cried a little as he worked on it for fifteen minutes before moving down to my lower back.

Jonjo came highly recommended by the hotel. He'd been doing this for a while . . . not inflicting pain on me you understand, but helping to keep bodies in shape. By the time he was done, the pain had gone. I handed over my money and headed back to the camper van, vowing never to have another massage. Not because it was bad, but because it felt as if I was floating. Nothing could ever make me feel as good as I did right then.

Over the following year or so I picked up only one injury, and it wasn't where you'd expect. I was in Navan, County Meath, when I helped push a car with a dead battery. I felt my right toe turn over as I pushed, but I felt no pain for weeks . . . not until I was up in County Donegal, playing Rosapenna. I played a shot and fell to the turf in agony.

'Bend over and touch your toes,' the physio said the following day, standing with her hands on hips in the Letterkenny Medical Centre.

I duly obliged.

'Well?' she asked.

'Well, what?'

'Are you going to bend over and touch your toes, or not?'

'What do you think I'm doing?' I replied.

She tutted. 'I see we have a problem.'

3

Fireworks of the North West

'It's good sportsmanship not to pick up lost balls while they are still rolling.'

MARK TWAIN

It had taken exactly one trip to derail my plans. As initial forays go, my travels through counties Waterford, Cork and Tipperary had been successful . . . with one caveat: the leaking roof. I could handle a temperamental fridge and eating the same food day after day, but a leaking roof was considerably more serious. A lot more depressing too. The leaks occurred mainly in the centre of the camper van, above the gas hob and above the sofa where I sat. The result was either a steady stream of drips that was easily avoided, or intermittent, stealth drips that were not. The water had also come through the TV aerial to soak my clothes on the shelves behind where the TV sat. Perhaps I wouldn't have minded so much if the TV had worked, but there was more cabling for one TV than for the entire media village at an Open Championship. And besides, the instruction manual was in Dutch.

33

I drove out to Inch, a twenty-minute drive up towards Arklow from my Wexford home, and left Rusty in the hands of the guys at East Coast Campers. They couldn't find a hole so they proceeded to tape up the entire roof, removing the air-conditioning unit at the same time.

While I waited for Rusty to be fixed, I reviewed the big trip I was set to embark on. I had my different routes charted on a large map of Ireland, and loops of colour turned the paper into a kaleidoscope that resembled the Olympic rings. The last time I'd used that many felt-tip pens I'd been in playschool.

I was heading to the northwest, slicing through the heart of Ireland, on the way to counties Donegal and Sligo. The N3 brushes past the Hill of Tara and Newgrange on its path through the Royal County. These are two of Ireland's most cherished sites and as I drove towards Kells I slipped off the motorway south of Navan town and went to enjoy the beauty that is the Hill of Tara. It was the most inspiring way I could think of to start a journey that would take in so much of Ireland. It is said that this was the ancient seat of power in Ireland, which pretty much described Rusty's current role, although without the power.

First up was Headfort Golf Club, on the outskirts of Kells. I'd had no problems parking overnight in the golf clubs along the south coast, but Rusty still raised an eyebrow or two. Later on my travels I had a few fraught moments with suspicious golfers or greenkeepers banging on doors and windows to inform me: 'you can't park here', followed by discussions as to who I was and phone calls to committee members who weren't best pleased at being disturbed at all hours of the night.

At Headfort I had my first encounter with the gardaí. The club was fine with me staying overnight but evidently one of the members wasn't. After a round on the New course in the morning, a sparkling parkland of lakes, woodland and islands, I returned to find a garda car circling the camper. It was doing slow loops as the passenger peered out the window. I hadn't reached them before they drove off, so I thought no more about it. Leaving the clubs and trolley outside I climbed in and made myself a sandwich. I had twenty minutes before I was due on the Old course so I sat on the steps, ate my lunch and enjoyed the surroundings.

A few minutes later the slow crunch of gravel was followed by the white nose of a car poking around the front of the camper van. Then the rest of the garda car appeared. What is it about being confronted by the law that makes every normal act so hard to perform? I had done nothing wrong and yet chewing my lunch had become difficult.

I tried to combine a wave with a casual nod and ended up hitting myself in the forehead with the sandwich. The car stopped in front of me and a window whirred down.

The garda's eyes went from me to the golf clubs, to my shoes and then to the camper.

'Are you a golfer?' he enquired.

Jeez, this lad was well trained.

'Earlier today, we received a report from a concerned citizen that a vehicle was seen behaving suspiciously in the vicinity of the Headfort Golf Club car park,' the garda continued.

In the garda manual on *How To Address The Public In As Many Words As Possible*, Rule 1B states that members of the Garda Síochána must use all the words they have at their disposal in a single sentence, in the style of an RTÉ news reporter but without moving their lips. According to the manual, a garda's pay and allowances are directly proportional to the number of words used. This fella was having a bumper month.

I cleared the air and allayed the fears of concerned citizens everywhere. Then I played the Old course, secure in the knowledge that Rusty would not be behaving 'suspiciously' in anyone's vicinity . . . at least not while I was on the golf course.

The route to the northwest took me to different courses across County Cavan, a landscape of rolling hills, forty shades of green and roads that gave the term 'pothole' new meaning. I fully understood Martin Hannigan's complaints. I'm surprised he had enough yellow paint to do the job.

Ireland's road difficulties aren't confined to potholes. No, we have another trick up our sleeves, one designed to confuse the bejaysus out of tourists and single men in camper vans. *Céad míle fáilte* is what Irish tourism is all about but that doesn't mean we make it easy to get around the country . . . and that's because, with barely a whiff of notice, we change the road number completely when you pass between Ireland and Northern Ireland.

After I left Slieve Russell Golf Club late one day I found myself drifting through the darkness on the R183. It's a country road, going to and coming from nowhere in particular, so who needs a fanfare that they're leaving one country to enter another? I do! With no warning, a roadside sign informed me that I was driving on the A34. No I'm bloody not, I thought. Where did the R183 go?

I had no idea what was going on when I rounded a corner to find the road soaked with light. A wooden shack, no more than a barn really, was buzzing with people. Cars were parked so haphazardly it was as if they'd been swept there by a flood. Men were skulking off towards the shack, casting glances over their shoulders at the sound of every passing vehicle. It was then that I realised I was in Northern Ireland, for the shack was selling fireworks. Fireworks are illegal in

Ireland, so punters simply drove a few hundred yards over the Border to satisfy the Hallowe'en cravings of their young ones. The gardaí, so eager to investigate suspicious vehicles in golf club car parks and caution men painting yellow circles on the road, didn't give a fiddlers about fireworks coming in to the country, and these folks, with their stacks of fireworks, had nothing to fear.

As it turned out, my trip into Northern Ireland lasted exactly one day. The following evening I left Enniskillen town and drove in to County Sligo, the A4 road morphing into the N16 at the border crossing of Belcoo.

Whether it's the good times or the bad times, there are two things the Irish are exceptionally talented at: getting married and having babies. Often at the same time. A wedding was in full swing at Castle Dargan when I arrived. The resort is tucked away in the countryside near Ballygawley, and I was here because Darren Clarke designed the golf course that forms part of the resort. I never saw the groom – then again, don't all the lads in suits look the same – but the bride and bridesmaids were glaringly obvious and loud. The party had taken over the hotel and there was no quiet corner, so I located the next best thing: a stool at the far end of the bar.

I soon found myself in conversation with Phil, a young man who looked bored out of his skin and a little too eager to get away from a girl I assumed was his date. His charcoal suit was a touch long in the sleeve, so his hands kept disappearing and then reappearing as he reached for his pint. I expected a bit of Tommy Cooper, especially since he was so keen to do a vanishing act on his girlfriend.

'Three years?' I queried, somewhat dumbstruck, when he told me how long he'd been courting Siobhan. He had just shooed her away after she'd found him, but hadn't even looked at her. In return she'd glared at me like I was trying to steal him from under her nose. He wasn't even my type.

Phil was already after a few and polished off another two pints while he countered my golfing quest with conquests of his own . . . mostly while he was dating Siobhan. He was a good-looking guy, tall and lean, and I could see why girls would fall for that sallow skin, brown eyes and boyish face. He was also an arrogant, misogynistic bollocks.

There was an announcement that the wedding dinner was about to be served, which was his cue to order another.

'What time are you playing in the morning?' he asked as he slid dangerously off his stool.

'Seven a.m.' I thought – I hoped – that would put him off.

'See you on the tee, so.'

I can't say I was that surprised when he failed to show and I spotted Phil in the restaurant after my round. There were several guests milling about but he was alone. His suit was still on and he looked like many a wrecked Irishman on a Sunday morning. The head was bowed, the hair dishevelled, the movements slow. The suit had endured a hard night too. Crumpled from top to bottom, it resembled an old accordion, and one that had been played badly for most of the night.

I could have played County Sligo Golf Club that same day – maybe I should have, given what was to follow – but the club, also known as Rosses Point, had a warm, inviting bar and spectacular views. And a Bridge Club that interrupted my evening's plans with their weekly game in the lounge. I finished my drink and slipped out to a forceful declaration of 'Three Hearts'.

I had been on the road for almost two weeks and the

October rain had yet to make an appearance. It made up for it that night and at about 5 a.m. I discovered that the lads from East Coast Campers had failed to repair the leak. I found it utterly depressing. It sapped my energy and motivation and the following morning, as the rain hammered down, I didn't even bother leaving Rusty to check on my tee time. I used my mobile phone to call the pro shop instead.

One of the great beauties of Ireland and her weather is the instant changes it can conjure up. At noon, the rain turned to sunshine and I stepped out of the van and watched the heavy clouds sweep their way across Drumcliff Bay, towards the Black Rock lighthouse. The sun fired up a rainbow and as I climbed the steep 2nd, it burned against the dark skies that hung over Benbulbin. It was the most striking sight I had seen and the 360-degree views were captivating. Benbulbin is a rock formation that possesses steep limestone walls and a plateau-like top. It is often compared to Capetown's Table Mountain, but Benbulbin has a menace about it, like it is ploughing through the landscape towards the ocean. And with the black clouds behind it, that menace – and beauty – was magnified.

I played on my own, the other golfers having fled with the rain, and I took my time on a course that changed pace and direction constantly but made my love for it grow deeper with every stride. Rosses Point is home to the amateur West of Ireland Championship. Winners include Padraig Harrington (1994), Rory McIlroy (2005 and 2006) and Shane Lowry (2008). Those are a few of the famous names on the cup but, as impressive as they are, they pale in comparison to Ireland's greatest amateur golfer, J. B. Carr, who won the championship twelve times between 1946 and 1971, and never lost a final.

There's another small piece of club history that few people are aware of. At some point during Carr's reign, three

Japanese businessmen came to Ireland to check on the progress of their company's Sligo factory. The factory was managed by a friend of my parents and when these three men indicated they wanted to play golf they were sent to Rosses Point.

On arriving at the golf club they tried to make their wishes known, but between their poor English and a strong Sligo accent, it proved a struggle. The Japanese finally pulled out their Irish punts and the Pro picked out the necessary notes. History doesn't relate how well the visitors played, but they enjoyed it so much that they came back to Ireland six months later, on the premise of visiting the factory once more. They arrived at Rosses Point and started handing over money but the Pro wasn't having any of it, pushing the money back at the men.

On returning to the factory they sat down with the manager. 'What,' they asked in faltering English, 'is Life Membership?'

This was the start of one of the most spectacular runs of golf I encountered, and there was no deliberate plan to do so. Over the coming weeks I would play fourteen links courses of different sizes and shapes, with different claims to fame and varying reputations.

I assumed that Strandhill Golf Club, my next stop, would be a poor relation of Rosses Point. I arrived late in the evening to an empty clubhouse and car park, and both were still empty the following morning as I stood on the 1st tee. The sun stayed low behind Knocknaree Mountain, upon which the tomb of Queen Meabh, the legendary Queen of Connacht, is said to reside. The mountain threw shadows across Ballysadare Bay strand, behind the opening green. The course is no less inspiring than Rosses Point, in its own unique way, and it has the advantage of boasting sea on two sides: Ballysadare Bay to the south and Sligo Bay to the west. The western beach has become increasingly popular with surfers and from the 7th tee you can watch them do their thing. The southern beach, on the other hand, is reserved for other activities. As I played alongside the beach, I felt the vibrations as two racehorses streaked past me at full gallop across the sand. Ears back, eyes wide, nostrils flared, and that was just the jockeys.

There is something otherworldly about playing first thing in the morning with no one else around. The course becomes your personal fiefdom, as if it had been created for you and you alone. Strandhill felt like that. The 5th hole flows over the most rugged and rollercoaster fairway I experienced and, with the early morning sun creating perfect light and shadow, I snapped a photograph back down the fairway and across to the Slieve Gamph Mountains. It was a perfect shot – one of the few I managed all day – and that image has adorned my golfing business card ever since.

I ended up rushing along the N59 to get to Enniscrone, or Inniscrone or Inishcrone. Take your pick, because the Irish don't make it easy for tourists. I may have mentioned this before. Road numbering and quality aside, we also like to mix up the spelling so that the name on the map does not always correspond to the name on the signpost. In a country where 'Bally' or 'Balli' appears in the name for hundreds of villages and towns, how would a non-English-speaking tourist cope with the sizeable difference between Enniscrone and Inishcrone? How many people have gone sailing by the turn-off? How many tee times have been missed?

I didn't miss mine, but I found myself on the tee with seven young guys who were on a stag party. Ronnie – the groom to be – asked if I'd make up the numbers so we could play a match. It turned out I was the lowest handicap by ten strokes, so a bidding war started over whose team I'd be on.

I ended up being traded for four pints. Not a bad trade I decided, although not as impressive as the two camels a friend of mine was offered in exchange for his new bride while on honeymoon in Egypt. He still keeps them in the back garden.

My partner for the afternoon was Paul, a non-golfer with the swing to prove it. Someone had chosen video clips of different golfers, cut out the relevant parts and then pasted them together to create the ugliest swing I had ever seen. By the time he was on his downswing, his golf club and arms had swung around most of his body while his hip gyrations would have made John Travolta proud. He had the last laugh, though, leaving his tee shot two inches from the cup on the par three 3rd. It had taken an indirect route mind you, flying well right of the target before ricocheting off something in the dunes and almost netting him the most unlikely hole-in-one.

'There are two other guys in the gang,' Paul told me on one of the tee boxes. 'They preferred to go fishing.'

One of the other lads yawned loudly.

'We're meeting up back in Ballina this evening if you want to come along for some pints.'

Paul told me that he worked in Dublin, selling drugs to doctors. The legitimate kind, he assured me.

'Sure, sure,' I replied, not believing a word of it. 'Do you get to play much golf?'

He laughed. 'You have seen my swing, right! I'd love to play more, but a wife and two-year-old boy make it impossible. I play twice a year if I'm lucky. This,' he said, gesturing to the deep, rolling dunes around us, 'this is my first round this year.' It was October.

I have found several of my friends play less and less as

family commitments take over. It doesn't help when a round of golf seems to be taking longer and longer. Anything inside four hours is a victory. I expect rounds to be three-and-a-half hours, even for a four-ball, because anything longer means the entire day gets lost.

Our Enniscrone round was long, but it was also loud, abusive and a heap of fun. A bit too much time spent in the rough looking for balls, and one of the guys was a touch too competitive for my taste – cheering an opponent's missed putt is not done, old boy – but it was a grand day thanks to the company and the exceptional golf course.

At the end of the round I checked with Steve, Ronnie's best man, if it was OK to tag along.

He gave me a long stare. 'How else are you going to buy the pints?'

The boys were staying in Ballina town, a few minutes' drive from the golf club, and their pub for the night was Murphy's. It's on Howley Street on the banks of the River Moy. It may be away from the buzz of the colourful town but it is popular. With its balconies and flowers spilling through the railings, it has a New Orleans touch to it.

There was even a decent-sized car park around back. I hadn't been able to keep up with the lads after they left the golf course, so they were already into their first pints by the time I arrived. It was after nine o'clock and my next round of golf was, conveniently, at Ballina in the morning.

I asked the barman if I could leave the camper van overnight.

'Your risk, mate,' he said in a perfect Aussie accent, sliding my pint across the bar. I found the guys and was introduced to the two fishermen, who hadn't caught a thing. Paul caught my eye and nodded towards the table beside us. Four pints of lager were bunched in a tidy square.

'Your fee for joining us today.'

'Fee? I thought I was traded for four pints.'

'Exactly,' said Steve, who was looming over my shoulder. 'Each member of the other team had to buy you a pint. Now drink up.'

Murphy's has an effortless warmth to it. Nothing fake, Aussie barmen aside, and the place was buzzing. It was even civilised until the nightclub kicked off.

I was older than the guys by about a decade, and dressed accordingly, so I felt out of place queuing to get into the club where kids were whipping out ID as proof they were over eighteen. The bouncer was the Australian from behind the bar.

'ID,' he said when I reached him.

'What? You can't be serious.'

His expression said he was. 'You're over age.'

'Over . . . what . . . I swear I'm not.'

'Look mate, no one under thirty wears a jumper like that to a nightclub.' He paused and then gave me a big smile. 'Go on, I'm kidding.'

These days when it comes to nightclubs I'm about as useful as a handbrake on a canoe – completely the wrong tool for the job – but I was rather fond of my yellow V-neck sweater.

Long Necks is everything I remembered and loved about Irish nightclubs. It had been a while since I'd been in a 'country' club, but all the essentials were there: the bar, the dance floor lower than the rest of the venue, the old lads leaning over the railing with their pints, ogling the young women who were dancing around handbags with perfect synchronisation, and the mouthy DJ who welcomed every guest by name and kept asking 'Do you remember this one?' before spinning a Duran Duran track from the Ice Age.

The others were off at the bar, leaving Paul and me to stare vacantly into the pit of debauchery that was the dance floor.

'Do you think their fathers know they're out dressed like that?' I asked.

Paul gave me a look and raised an eyebrow.

'Jesus,' I muttered. 'I'm getting old.'

The others returned, setting themselves up along the railing for some talent-spotting.

An hour later the lights dimmed.

'It's time to slow things down a little,' the DJ mumbled breathlessly into his microphone.

We had reached the bottom-of-the-barrel, nightclub slow set. Yes, the mating ritual had begun as the males descended onto the floor and claimed a woman, any woman, for the slow set shift that has almost single-handedly led to the never-ending baby boom in this country.

I was left at the railing with Ronnie, who was under strict instructions to stay away from the women and guard the pints. Groom-to-be he may have been, but even he looked sick to his stomach when 'Lady In Red' kicked in.

It took me a couple of days to recover from that night, by which time I was in Castlebar, County Mayo's largest town. The morning was accompanied by a mist so deep and lifeless you could have leant out of the window and cut off a piece. Shadows of people slid by and lights from passing cars reached only a few feet into the haze.

Castlebar Golf Club is a couple of miles outside the town and the mist was less dense, but even so, Gerry's appearance came as a shock. He materialised out of the mist, from the left of the 13th fairway, walking straight towards me as if he knew exactly where I'd be. Over one shoulder he carried a bag with a bare handful of clubs. He stopped and looked at me.

'Not often I see folk on the course at this hour.' He nodded to himself and took a few more steps. 'I don't recognise you.'

I introduced myself and explained that I played a lot of my golf early in the morning.

'Good, good,' he replied. 'I'm Gerry.' He looked at the ball on the fairway and glanced back to where the tee box punctured the mist. 'Is that your drive, son?'

I guessed Gerry was in his eighties. He had a thin face that matched his frame and he carried his clubs effortlessly. The flat cap of garish colours that he wore reminded me of the pizza I had eaten the previous week: utterly tasteless.

'It is,' I replied.

Quick as you like, he rolled the bag off his shoulder and had it propped against his leg. 'How's about a wee game?' he ventured. 'Four holes straight up. Five quid. We'll finish up on 16. What do you say?'

The month before I had been in Rosslare Golf Club on the southeastern tip of Ireland. Sitting in the changing rooms of one of the island's unheralded links, I watched a man of considerable age hobble in.

'Are you all right, Arthur?' another old man asked him. 'Is our match still on?'

Arthur groaned as he sat down and put on his shoes. 'Of course it's on, and I want back that €5 you won last month . . . but between my cataracts, angina, bad knees and gout I really don't want to spend any more time on the course than is necessary.' He stood up and slapped the other man on the shoulder. 'So it's just as well I've been cut two shots.'

He guffawed laughing as he headed out, leaving his opponent muttering obscenities.

The experience made me wary of old men prepared to gamble. 'Bit early for throwing money about, isn't it?' I asked Gerry.

'Pah! Never too early, sonny. Never. I'll drop one here and we'll start.'

'What about handicaps?' I asked, rather incredulously as he took a ball and let it fall.

He gave me a grand smile that crinkled his entire face all the way up to his eyes. 'All the same to me. How about no strokes, man-to-man? Reckon you can beat an old fella, or do you want me to give you a stroke a hole, sonny?' He winked a watery blue eye at me.

It was a classic 'chicken' challenge and I stepped back and gestured to his ball. 'Work away,' I said, knowing full well I was playing straight into his hands.

He investigated the contents of his bag, one that dated back to the nineteenth century, and selected a wood that looked just as old.

And that was the second shock of the morning: he had a swing uglier than Paul's. He took his stance like a man stepping out into a force-ten gale while his dog fought with his trouser cuff to dissuade him. The right leg twitched and shook during a backswing better designed for chopping logs, and then bounced as he made contact. The follow-through twisted into a windmill of wood chippings and the leg finally ceased. It may not have been a thing of beauty but, as Eamonn Darcy will testify, the swing matters little if the clubface aligns itself perfectly inches before impact.

Gerry's ball shot forward with a mighty crack, straight towards the green. He nodded with satisfaction and replaced the wood in the bag.

'Ready when you are.'

I hit my second and then we waded off through the mist to do battle.

Gerry was a character and a real Irishman. A sweeping generalisation it may be, but I've always found that the Irish play things close to their chest with strangers. We're friendly and hospitable – *ceád mile fáilte* and all that – and we have a great reputation for it, yet it's skin deep until we get to know you.

We talked about a lot of things, but whenever I asked him about himself, Gerry deflected the question. Beautifully done of course, but there was no getting through that friendly armour.

I won the hole with a bogey when Gerry failed to get out of a bunker, and then won 14 as well. I was dormie two, and yet I was still waiting for Gerry to turn it on. He never did. What he loved was the thrill of the competition, the excitement of a well-struck shot – be it his or mine – and the apprehension of standing over a critical putt.

'Do you know our famous politicians in these parts?' he asked as we stood on the par-three 16th, our last hole. He crouched over the ball as the dog returned to tug at his trousers, and knocked the ball into the water well right of the green.

'Hmmm,' he muttered with disappointment, no doubt seeing a potential double-or-quits challenge evaporate before his eyes. 'Beverley Cooper Flynn. She's the one who gets everyone in a tizzy.'

We launched into a discussion on the Irish economy, politics and politicians, and I told him about the framed photograph of Beverley and then Taoiseach, Bertie Ahern, hanging in the men's changing rooms at Claremorris.

Gerry went so red in the face I thought his head would explode.

'Do you know where the term politics comes from?' he spat, after a tirade against Bev and Bertie.

I suspected it was Greek, but I said I didn't.

Gerry gave a chuckle. 'From "poly", meaning many, and "tics", meaning blood-sucking insects.' He threw his head back as he laughed, tipping his golf bag and clubs onto the fairway.

The mist had drifted off, but the heavy moisture remained and Gerry's clubs were soaked.

'How old are they?' I asked, picking up a flat blade iron with a wooden shaft. The grooves in the clubface had almost disappeared.

'They were my father's.'

Clearly Gerry wasn't keeping pace with the world of technology. I hadn't seen a wooden shaft since my grandfather's day, and here was Gerry playing with nothing but. The head on his 3 wood was so small and dark, it could have been mistaken for a hybrid.

Ignoring technology is no bad thing. Too many golfers rely on it to correct the faults in their game. Every year new clubs, new balls, new whatever come forth to add distance and/or to create a bigger and more forgiving sweet spot. When I first picked up a driver, thirty years ago, I couldn't use it for peanuts, every mis-hit sending those painful vibrations through my fingers and arms. Today, I own a driver with a head the size of a small country. It's almost impossible to duff a ball.

Watching Gerry's inelegant swing but perfect timing made me realise it's about working with what you have and doing your best to master your clubs.

On the green, Gerry handed over the cash even as I insisted on not taking it.

'Come on, come on,' he said, looking towards the club-house at a couple of elderly gents preparing to set off. 'Hurry up and take the money. I can see I'm going to win it back soon enough.'

Half an hour's drive to the east is Charlestown, a small town on the N5 that is home to Knock Airport, or Ireland West Airport Knock as it is now memorably named. It has had a string of names since Monsignor James Horan was responsible for the airport opening in 1986. That inability to find a lasting name reflects an inability to understand why or how the airport was built in the first place. A vision of the Blessed Virgin Mary in 1879 led to the establishment of Knock Shrine, which led to a giant black slab of tarmac being laid in the middle of a bog. If I had a vision of Charlie Haughey, could I expect a giant brown envelope to land in my back yard?

It was at Knock Airport that my dad and I collected his cousin, John, some years before. I had arranged for us to play at Carne Golf Club in Belmullet, some 100 kilometres away to celebrate my dad's birthday. The town is in the very northwest corner of Mayo, where a narrow spit of land refuses to release what would be a seahorse-shaped island.

It is difficult to describe Carne Golf Club in one word, but 'heaven' just about covers it. This is Ireland's, and possibly one of the world's, greatest golfing adventure. We played twice because with a course this far from anywhere and this good it's a prerequisite. The dunes are big. In fact, they're twice as big as big, with views all around and the kind of wind that could pick you up off the green and deposit you back on the tee . . . and you wouldn't complain one bit. That is what you'll have to contend with because Carne flows around and over dunes that must have been the playground of giants.

On our second day I insisted that Dad take a buggy so he and John could share it. Fat lot of use that did, because I ended up driving it on my own most of the time. Dad strode around Carne like it was his back garden. Besides, a buggy here is a liability: some of the slopes up, down and across the dunes are so steep that you could tip a buggy over. I waited until the 18th before I tried it.

Belmullet was too far for me to journey on this trip and I had such fond memories that I could remember the course as if I had played it yesterday.

Much of County Sligo promotes itself as Yeats Country, but if there is a piece of land that undeniably belongs to William Butler Yeats, one of Ireland's greatest writers, it is a six-foot-deep plot in Drumcliff churchyard. Ten minutes to the north of Sligo town, in the shadow of Benbulbin, the church and graveyard sit beside the road. The small car park was full of cars and tourists as Rusty and I sailed by. We were heading farther north still, for the village of Grange and the evocatively named L3203 road that winds its way towards the sea. It leads to one of Ireland's most beautiful beaches, a spit of land drenched in deep golden sand and dunes, curling for 2 miles into the Atlantic Ocean.

I discovered Streedagh Strand purely by accident several years ago, when my wife and I were staying in Enniscrone. After visiting Sligo town, Drumcliff and W. B. Yeats, we ended up following country lanes until we reached this deserted paradise. Rolls of white-tipped waves flowed onto the sand and we walked alone as Benbulbin's stern gaze spilled down its buttressed forehead. On this visit I pulled the camper van into the car park – no more than an extension of the beach – where three cars and a horsebox demonstrated a significant increase in the beach's popularity.

Apart from four surfers jogging towards the water, there wasn't a soul to be seen. How could a beach this perfect have next to no one on it? I walked along the water line, letting water bubble over my feet and the smell of the ocean fill my lungs. It was intoxicating.

Before I knew it, I was a mile down the beach and utterly alone. It was at that point that I realised something rather surprising: the water was warm. I rolled up the legs of my trousers and waded out until it was up to my knees. Still warm. Deliciously so. I appreciate that everyone's definition of warmth is different, but for an Irish beach the water was caressingly tepid. I didn't have any swimming trunks or a towel but it was a sunny day – I'd dry.

Back on the beach I stripped down to my boxers. I waded back into the clear water expecting my mind to see reason, but logic had taken the day off. I swam out farther until the chill became obvious. The top layer was cosy but it turned cold fast and I was beginning to lose the sensation in my fingers and toes.

I walked out of the water and was approaching my clothes when two horses and their riders crested the dune right in front of me. They were as surprised to see me as I was them. I waved awkwardly at the two women who stared as they galloped past.

'Nice shorts,' one of them yelled, and they burst into laughter.

I looked down. My boxers had gone completely see-through. Fortunately, the cold meant there was nothing to see.

There are many beautiful beaches along this stretch of coastline and Mullaghmore, close to Castlegal, is the most well known. Being so far north, they don't attract the same numbers as those on the west coast, but that means far fewer people with whom to share these idyllic stretches of sand.

Bundoran is still farther to the east of Streedagh Strand and Mullaghmore. It is a popular tourist destination, but it's not what you'd call attractive. A main street flanked with arcade emporiums and trinket shops didn't instil much confidence and I drove through quickly, in search of the golf club. I found it soon enough down one of the side streets, wrapped around the Great Northern Hotel. Even from the side street you can see that the exposed landscape of Bundoran Golf Club is going to be brutal. This is where you come for a true education in the art of links golf and golfers have been doing so for 120 years.

The elegant links of the Donegal Golf Club, set on the isolated Murvagh Peninsula, could not have been a more different links experience to Bundoran. This had an idyllic setting and a panorama of views that were bursting with colour in every direction, from the Blue Stack Mountains to the north to the surroundings of Donegal Bay. The only thing marring it was the body of the dead woman.

'Did I hear you right?' I asked Eamonn as we walked down the 1st hole. 'They found a body by the green?'

John was on the other side of me. 'Under it. When Pat Ruddy was here, redoing the greens, they found a woman's body under the 1st.' He gestured to the green we were making towards.

'What did the gardaí have to say?'

'Not a lot. They weren't interested.'

I stopped in my tracks. 'What? I don't follow.'

'The body had been there a long time,' John said over his shoulder.

'But not long enough to interest the archaeologists,' Eamonn added.

I expected a plaque by the green, but there was nothing. The poor woman had the ignominy of having no one who was remotely interested in her.

A little bit of intrigue goes a long way at golf clubs, but

the body under the 1st green was peanuts compared to what was to come later on the trip.

Eamonn and John were in their seventies but you wouldn't know it to see them out striding the links. Playing off 6 and 10 handicaps they showed me a thing or two about how to play links golf. Punched irons, cutting shots into the wind, hitting a 5 iron from 40 yards. It was one of the joys of meeting different golfers. You learn a lot and you laugh a lot, which is what golf should be about.

After the round I showered and headed up to the lounge, looking forward to a hot meal and a sociable chat. Instead, I got a barmaid looking at her watch, telling me that despite it being a Saturday night the clubhouse was closing in five minutes. It was 7 p.m.

I had anticipated many a night in a clubhouse bar, drinking and socialising with a grand crowd of like-minded souls. But, thanks to the smoking ban of 2004, and random breath-testing in 2006, I realised this wasn't to be. Clubhouses shut their doors once it got dark, which meant 7 p.m. or earlier. With not another living soul for a couple of miles of the Murvagh Peninsula, I ended up sitting in the camper alone, feeling both depressed and lonely. I cooked pasta from a ripped packet and tomato sauce from a pot that told me the Best Before Date had passed the previous day. How fitting.

I typed up my reviews until the battery on my laptop died. That got me to 8 p.m. I read a book, shaved, clipped my toenails, sorted through my sock drawer and tried to keep myself occupied . . . by which stage it was 9 p.m. I gave up and went to bed.

'Dear Christ,' I yelled, slamming on the brakes. The advantage of an early night meant that I was wide awake at 6 a.m., which was just as well. I had left the Murvagh Peninsula minutes before in inky morning darkness, heading north towards Donegal town on an empty road. The last thing I expected to see was a woman standing in the middle of the road, arms raised, flagging me down.

She wasn't budging, which is more than I can say for anything that wasn't tied down in the camper van. Sharp stops don't suit camper van life.

'Hello,' I said, sticking my head out of the window. 'Are you all right?'

'I'll be fine,' she shot back, 'once you give me a lift into town. I'm late for work.'

I directed her around to the side door and moved a few of the things that had accumulated in the passenger seat in the preceding seconds – a saucepan, a baseball cap and half the contents of the bin.

'Not exactly easy getting in, is it?' she remarked sharply, clambering through the door. I hadn't lowered the step for her so I said nothing. She was a small woman, probably in her seventies. It was difficult to tell with the floral scarf wrapped so tightly around her head that her face looked like it had been planted in a rose bed.

'You can sit up front, with me.' I gestured to the passenger seat.

She squeezed through the gap, keeping a firm eye on me and kicked my trolley away from her feet. 'Drive straight on. I'll tell you when to turn.'

Yes ma'am. So much for not giving any more lifts to hitchhikers. Then again, this was no hitchhiker. I had a bona fide Irish mammy on board. I was considering my opening conversational gambit when she got in first.

'Do you have children?'

'No,' I replied, keeping my eyes on the road, wary of

Donegal's notorious boy racers and old folk attempting to stop moving vehicles with the power of thought. I glanced to my right. Hold on, could this be Yoda's mum?

'I have twelve,' she said, and proceeded to tell me their names, ages, spouses' names, their children's names, where they went to school, who did what, with whom, where and how often. Sadly, Yoda wasn't mentioned.

It was like winding up a toy and letting it go. Generalisation it may be, but an Irish mammy in full flow is as unstoppable as the tide, and a lot more wearing. I didn't get a word in.

We were somewhere in the middle of the clan when I saw signposts up ahead, directing me off to Donegal town.

'Daniel works in the factory. He's a manager you know. His wife's lovely but no children yet. Then there's Barbara, who's married to Joe, you know. Left here. He's an accountant. Left, yes left. Here. Left,' she barked loudly, disturbing my catatonic state.

I turned left.

'It's a small office, only three of them, but Joe's the boss. Seamus is their boy, seven now, go straight on at the lights, OK, and in school. Not that he likes it, but who liked school, you know, all them know-it-all teachers acting superior. Sure, I didn't. Turn right, all that nonsense you had to learn. That's me up ahead, pull in here, that'll do fine. He's already playing the hurling.'

She was still talking as she climbed out of the camper van and walked off up the road.

Suffering a mild case of earache, I retraced my steps and drove through the town, laughing at those Irish people who manage to talk non-stop without ever pausing for breath. They fill their sentences with *OKs*, *you knows* and *likes*, so no one else can get a word in edgeways. They have some kind of fear that they may suddenly no longer be in charge of the conversation, so they rush their words and sentences into one huge soliloquy that, in reality, doesn't need another participant.

I looked for signs to the fishing village of Killybegs, farther along the coast. The sun had arrived, spilling its light over the landscape, turning the evocatively named Blue Stack Mountains into a bruised patchwork of colours, dappled by cloud and shadow. It was a beautiful morning as I skirted the mountains to the west and I found my foot pressing down on the accelerator, eager to reach Narin & Portnoo on such a gorgeous autumn day.

The golf club is not the easiest place to find, even though I could see fairways and greens coming down into Narin. As I began the descent towards the village it felt like the hillside was tipping everything into the sea. The only thing on level ground was the mobile home park, through which I drove to reach the clubhouse.

The beauty of the day made it special, but Narin & Portnoo Golf Club is also one of Ireland's best-kept secrets. It is a stunning links that starts simply and then explodes from halfway along the 5th hole. Somewhere ahead there was another golfer who had arrived after me. I watched him jump from the car, stare at my golf clubs lying on the ground and then race to the tee, practically falling out of his shoes as he scuttled his way to tee off before me.

Every club has its early morning brigade, golfers who get upset if they're not out first and see it as their right. That said, there aren't many such golfers who then hit eight drives off the tee. As I watched him hit ball after ball, I settled down to breakfast. Leftovers of pasta was not what I had in mind but it was all I had and I wasn't going anywhere soon.

Surprisingly, I never saw the golfer again, but on the 8th

tee I ran into someone else. A man was searching for golf balls. Martin Whelan, who is in his late seventies, is the club's longest-serving member. We chatted about Narin and he pointed to the small island in the bay.

'That's Inishkeel Island. The village has a barbecue there every summer. People go over for the day. You can walk across to it at certain times of year.'

Looking at the currents that twisted the water into lines of angry white foam between the beach and the island, it was hard to believe.

Inishkeel is a National Monument, St Conal founding a monastery there in the sixth century. The remains of two twelfth-century churches are still there today and you can see them from the golf course.

We discussed how the new course design would make Narin & Portnoo a must-visit destination.

'Those three back-to-back par fives make it too difficult for me, now,' Martin said. 'It went from a par sixty-nine to seventy-three in one go.'

'And you lost the cows as well, I believe.'

Martin nodded. 'That we did. No sense upgrading the course if you're asking visitors to play through the cowpats.'

Cattle roamed here freely enough until 2002. They were removed, along with the electric fencing around greens, before the course upgrade began in 2004. I told Martin about my Barley Cove adventures as a boy, hitting a shot off a cowpat.

Martin laughed. 'Many was the time I faced a similar dilemma, but I always took the free drop. If you still want the full experience, you need to head to Mulranny, north of Westport. A lovely little nine-hole links with cattle and sheep aplenty.'

Neither Martin nor I had a care in the world and we

chatted for a long time. We couldn't have picked a better spot because this is quite probably the most scenic hole on the entire island.

'You see Mount Errigal over there?' Martin pointed at a distant, sugar-dusted peak. 'It was at the foot of that mountain that my father and mother met. He was one of the first gardaí in the State, in 1922, and Gweedore was his first posting. His last posting, too! My mother was from the nearby village of Dunlewy and this is where they stayed.'

The Anglo-Irish Treaty was signed by the Irish and British governments in December 1921, giving rise to the Irish Free State. The Civic Guard was formed in 1922, and this became the Garda Síochána in 1923. The *How To Address The Public In As Many Words As Possible* manual quickly followed.

Narin & Portnoo Golf Club inspired me. I was utterly in love with it and it reinforced my belief that Donegal is one of the island's most beautiful counties. It rarely gets the recognition it deserves. Its glittering coastline is matched by the mountains and lakes that lace the interior. From Narin I headed east, on a steep and winding road that slid between the Blue Stack Mountains to the south and the Derryveagh Mountains to the north. From Glenties to Letterkenny there were exactly three cars on the road as I drove across the barren landscape – I know this because all three got stuck behind me.

I was exactly halfway through my fourteen-links-course extravaganza and, after a day in the town of Letterkenny, I steered farther north towards Downings, a small community that has thrived on the back of the holiday home boom and the Rosapenna Hotel and Golf Resort. Old Tom Morris came here in the 1890s to design the golf course. This was added to in 2004, when Pat Ruddy designed a second course – Sandy Hills – through Sheep Haven Bay's biggest dunes. It is big and muscular, drenched in grasses that flash silver in the wind. I played both courses alone because there was no one else on the golf course. An empty golf course is such a rarity and such a treat that most golfers would embrace those quiet moments with delight. Normally I did the same, but there was something eerie about Rosapenna. How could courses this brilliant not be packed with golfers? I wanted to ask when I got back to the clubhouse, but the place was closed.

Across Mulroy Bay and Broad Water, Portsalon is another wonderful Donegal links, where the sea dances along the long stretch of Ballymastocker Strand that embraces the bay, and Knockalla Mountain runs along the skyline.

Golfers are often conflicted in the parkland versus links debate. For me there is no debate because links is the origin of the game. Don't get me wrong, I love parkland golf, but links is raw, emotive, hair-on-your-chest golf. Just because you hit a perfect shot doesn't mean you'll get the perfect result. Links fairways and greens are fickle creatures, embracing you with open arms one shot, then dismissing your ball with a back-handed slap the next, to send your ball into the rough or a bunker that had never looked in play when the ball first took flight. I love that unpredictability and Portsalon delivered it in spades.

As at Rosapenna, there wasn't another body on the course, which is more than can be said for what's under it . . . under the 18th to be precise.

The number of bodies remains to be confirmed, but the story dates back 200 years, to 4 December 1811. A British ship named *HMS Saldanha* sank in Lough Swilly, near the beach beneath what is now the golf course. Over 250 lives were lost and it was one of the greatest sea tragedies recorded. Rocks near Fanad Head to the north were the cause of the disaster but the ship was blown south where she finally ran aground. The storm was so violent that all lives were lost.

The captain and his parrot survived briefly, but both suffered undignified deaths. First to die was the captain, William Pakenham, who made it to shore where locals tried to revive him by pouring poitín down his throat. Accustomed as he might have been to rum, the poitín proved too much and killed him, right there on the sand. The parrot lasted a few days longer before a local farmer decided it was worth shooting. On a collar around its neck were inscribed the words 'Captain Pakenham of His Majesty's Ship Saldanha'.

The captain received his own burial plot in Rathmullan Priory burial ground, but many of the sailors were placed in a mass grave under Portsalon's 18th fairway.

There is no record of the parrot's burial. I imagine the farmer ate it.

Fanad Head lighthouse was built in response to the disaster and its beacon first lit up Lough Swilly's dark waters on St Patrick's Day 1816, five years after the tragedy.

Over the years bones have been found on the golf course and, not surprisingly for a county which resorts to poitín in difficult situations, there have been numerous tales of ghostly sailors walking the roads or trying to enjoy a free round on the links.

Captain William Pakenham came from famous Irish stock, but it was his brother-in-law whom history remembers most: he was Sir Arthur Wellesley, who became the Duke of Wellington, victor of one of the greatest battles in history, at Waterloo, in 1815.

From Portsalon, the Inishowen Peninsula is a mere few hundred metres across Lough Swilly. By road, it is many miles farther. I took the coast road back to Letterkenny, passing through Rathmullan and Ray, where I had spent some of my early childhood. It is all picture-postcard stuff and Donegal is such a beautiful and large place that you could come here on holiday for the rest of your life and never go to the same place twice. Nor would you ever get bored of the scenery and hospitality, as I was discovering every day.

Ballyliffin was where I was headed. The story of the club's rise to fame is the stuff of a Hollywood blockbuster. This small, quaint links, built by the members with one tractor and one mower, found itself in dire straits and close to insolvency in the early 1990s. Then a white knight arrived (that would be Nick Faldo, the world's greatest golfer of the time), and things started to change because Faldo told the world about brilliant Ballyliffin. In fact, he wanted to buy the course but the members weren't prepared to sell. There is a raw beauty to this place, with brutally shorn mountains around you and the dark shadow of Glashedy Rock rising up from the Atlantic Ocean.

I didn't get to enjoy the Glashedy course quite as much as I should have. After playing the front nine at a steady pace, I stood on the 10th tee at 5.10 p.m. in the gathering gloom. I decided to continue but realised by the 13th that I'd made a daft decision. I could still see but I was a long way from the only light source in the area, namely the clubhouse. And between me and the clubhouse were dunes that could swallow a man whole. Lost on a windswept links, in the dark, was not an attractive proposition so I started to run between shots. By the 16th all I had to aim at was a shadow of a fairway, dark dunes looming alongside; by the 18th I had to hit my shot at the clubhouse because it was the only thing left that I could see. I probably set a speed record to cover the back nine . . . and my scorecard read one over for the last six holes. I could see more night golf in my future.

The clubhouse was busy, which was a refreshing change. A large society had been playing the Old Course and there was a good crowd in the bar. Unfortunately, I ended up next to the drunk. He was a young guy with a tightly-shaved head that accentuated his jug-like ears. The song he was booming out was not one I recognised.

'I've got drink all over my face . . . I've got drink all over my face.'

That seemed to be the sum total of the lyrics. He started again, poking a couple of the other lads and urging them to join in. They didn't, but that didn't stop him. On he went. I thought someone would tell him to shut up, but the only time he did was when he stopped to knock back the contents from his glass.

The Irish love a drink. We are known for our alcohol consumption and it has long been a national stereotype. Ten, fifteen pints are nothing to some of these lads. Visit any city centre on a Friday night and they all come out to play . . . or, given the number of fights that ensue, maybe you should stay at home instead. How they manage to swing a fist or a boot with all that liquid threatening to topple them is beyond me, but then I've never been a big drinker. My tolerance is pitifully low. During my twenties I once drank six pints at my local and was so incapacitated that the cleaner found me asleep in a cubicle of the men's toilets the following morning. She thought I was dead. So did I.

When Paul pointed to those four pints on the table of Murphy's in Ballina, I was filled with dread. Instead of seeing glasses filled with lager, I saw myself curled up on the floor of the camper van, asking that age old question of 'why?' while simultaneously placing my head inside the fridge because sticking one's face against something cold is the universal solution for stopping your insides from becoming outsides. As a technique, it's badly flawed.

'I've got drink all over my face . . .'

The lad in Ballyliffin wasn't giving up. He just went on and on, a bit like *The X Factor*.

I didn't know his song, nor did I join in but I was sorely tempted to contribute my own pint to the proceedings. Some drunks can be a hoot and some can be obnoxious boors. I was having no difficulty deciding which category this lad was in.

Ballyliffin is only a forty-minute drive from Malin Head, Ireland's most northerly point. Some years ago I sat on the Head's clifftops, known as Banba's Crown, and watched the sun set across the North Atlantic. With the winds that hammer the coastline it is not what you'd call a peaceful spot, but it does replenish the soul knowing that the next landfall to the north is the Arctic.

I played the Old Course the following morning before continuing my navigation of Inishowen by heading to Buncrana, home to one of Ireland's oldest golf courses and a founding member of the Golf Union of Ireland: North West Golf Club.

The battle that links courses face day after day is a brutal one. Dunes are meant to shift, no matter what Donald Trump thinks. That's their nature and coastal locations are always going to be pounded by the ocean. North West was established in 1891, and it has been battling the elements ever since. It has not been a successful fight. Over the last 120 years the ocean has taken a few football fields of land. Combined with the main road squeezing it from the other side, the golf course has been getting gradually smaller, to the point that two holes heading back and forth practically share the same fairway. Boulders now man the defences and the erosion has stopped, but it has left behind a tight course.

It remains a fine old links and Eugene, the secretary manager, had set himself the task of arranging for me to play with some locals. As it turned out, one of those locals was him.

We were teamed together against Patsy and John, and the betting started in earnest on the 1st tee.

'Twenty, twenty, twenty?' suggested Patsy.

'How about fifty, fifty, fifty?' countered John.

The wind was up, whipping in off Lough Swilly and tugging at trouser legs so they flapped around our ankles.

Eugene was shaking his head. 'Lads, I think we can stretch to a euro on the front, back and overall, don't you?'

The other two agreed, somewhat reluctantly I might add, which was ironic seeing as Eugene and I had to fork out €3 a piece after putting in a miserable display of golf. But it was an entertaining round, the kind that makes golf worth playing, with lots of chit-chat, insults and laughter whenever a bad shot was struck.

And so it continued in the clubhouse. Non-golfers often scoff at golf as a sport. It's too elitist, it takes too long and it doesn't require much energy they claim. Yes, there is some truth to those arguments, but it is by far the most friendly sport. What other game allows you to chat with your companions the entire time you're playing? Golf is so much more than swinging a club at a little white ball and strolling around manicured landscapes. It is an opportunity to release stress, relax, talk out your problems, catch up with friends, get gentle exercise and have a great laugh . . . which is where my round at North West came up trumps.

I spent a long time in the cosy bar soaking up the atmosphere, among other things, before leaving Inishowen and driving south for Londonderry or Derry or L'Derry or Stroke City. The place has more names than Knock Airport.

Whatever its name, it is Northern Ireland's second city and one of the island's most historic. The city boasts a walled walkway at its centre that dates back to the seventeenth century, but a monastic settlement was first established here as far back as 546AD.

History is not my strong suit. I did love the subject once

but by secondary school I had a new teacher who would make Professor Snape look joyful. That imperious look and swirling gown had been mastered long before Harry Potter came along. I hated his classes. But History was divided into two subjects, with Irish History requiring its own teacher. Mr Connor could not have been more different: he was a small man, both in stature and in nature. He was weak and mild, so we were brutal and cruel. He was mincemeat at the hands of sixteen-year-olds.

One of the boys, Angus, who had as much interest in education as a duck has in politics, was a particular thorn in Mr Connor's side. He stood up in the middle of class one day, walked to the back of the room, opened a window and climbed out. Moments later there was a knock on the door and Angus walked in.

'Sorry I'm late,' he said to rapturous applause from the class before taking his seat.

Mr Connor didn't say a word so other boys started doing the same thing. He lasted about six weeks.

My knowledge of Irish history has been hazy ever since.

'Can I ask you,' I said while I was facing Roisin across the City of Derry Golf Club bar, 'what's the deal with Derry versus Londonderry?'

She sucked in her breath as she handed over my pint. 'Well now,' she said, giving an exaggerated glance in both directions. I say exaggerated because the bar was empty.

'How long have you got?' Roisin was a dark-haired young woman, with an easy smile that must have sold pints by the truckload. 'The thing is, when you're having a conversation about the city, you say "Londonderry" the first time and thereafter you only say "Derry".'

'But the county is Derry,' I said. 'Surely that'll confuse. What if I'm talking about the city but then want to talk about the county as well?'

'Then you have to be clever and remember to say "Derry City" or "Derry District".'

'What's District got to do with it?'

She sighed and leaned on the bar. 'The District is also called Londonderry or Derry.'

I opened my mouth and then closed it again. This was getting me nowhere.

'It depends on whether you're a Unionist or a Nationalist,' Roisin added. 'Unionists call it Londonderry, Nationalists call it Derry. If you want to play it safe, try avoiding either name altogether.'

Try putting all that in a tourist guide. And if you do, I suggest you add a mention about the golf club's showers.

After my round the next morning I pushed open the door to the showers and stepped into the dark. There were no windows and no light switch either, but the lights flickered on automatically to reveal four cubicles against the far wall. I chose the right-hand one and was midway through washing my hair when the lights flicked off. I was in complete blackness, the kind you can actually feel.

'Hello?' I called out.

No reply. The water was still running so I called out more loudly.

Nothing. I twigged that the lights were controlled by motion sensors so I eased forward and opened the cubicle door, assuming the lights would come back on. They didn't.

I cursed and tried to step out of the shower. Shampoo was running down my face and I paid more attention to clearing it from my eyes than where I was going. My foot slapped into the cubicle step, my right toe taking the punishment.

Now I was hopping mad with soap in my eyes and in pain. I had no idea what was ahead of me so I was waving one arm in front like a tentacle and one overhead like a drowning man. My toe was in agony so I stopped in what I assumed was the middle of the room. It was still total darkness and I started jumping up and down on one leg, waving my arms like windmills in a desperate attempt to attract the sensor's attention.

That was the exact moment the door opened and the lights came on.

What the man standing in the doorway must have thought upon seeing a tubby, naked, balding man covered head to toe in soap performing some perverted version of *Riverdance*, I cannot imagine, but as he reeled backwards in horror I was fairly sure he'd need counselling for the next twenty years. I'm still waiting for the bill.

The A5 road led south to Strabane, along the path of the River Foyle, and then on to Newtownstewart, staying west of the Sperrin Mountains.

I leaned through the doorway of the Newtownstewart Golf Club office to introduce myself to Lorraine, the manager, and to check it was OK to stay overnight. As our conversation continued there was a scrape of a chair and a woman in her fifties pushed back to eye me up.

'Oh yes,' she said with a smirk to Lorraine, 'he'll do nicely.' She turned to me. 'Are you coming to the show?'

Lorraine had mentioned during our phone calls that there would be a Ladies Fashion Show on the night I'd be staying. I had thought nothing of it at the time, but now I felt a sense of dread. Lorraine was giving me a look that said 'be careful' so I muttered that I might pop in for a drink.

The woman, still wearing a big grin, paused to consider my reply. 'You realise,' she said slowly, 'that there won't be any other men around, so if you don't come in you might have a queue of ladies outside your camper van looking for some night-time entertainment.'

I hadn't realised any such thing. I can play Bridge and shuffle my way through some ballroom dancing, but I didn't think that was the kind of 'entertainment' she was referring to. I spent the evening squirrelled away in a corner of the bar, hiding behind my book and nursing a solitary pint. I feared I would need several more, but a trip to the bar meant being out in the open and in plain sight of the hordes of women who were being shown the latest fashions.

Eventually I slipped out and returned to Rusty. I locked doors, closed curtains, turned off lights, inserted earplugs and prayed. I only felt safe when I crossed the Border into County Monaghan the next day.

It was a wet and miserable day as I drove in to Monaghan town, the kind when a golfer is thinking about the 19th as he walks onto the 1st tee. A small row of shops offered respite from the elements and I raced for the shop with the fading photographs in the window. If I'd stopped to look I would have seen models displaying hairstyles that went out of fashion in the 1980s, but it's not like I was after anything complicated.

I was the lone customer in the brightly-lit hairdressers. The floors, walls and ceiling were white; everything else was black. The hairdresser, dressed in black, blended right in. She was a young woman and looked normal enough, until my eyes drifted down to her bare feet, which were encased in bright green flip-flops.

'Good morning,' she said, tapping the chair in front of her.

Don't ask me why but the flip-flops worried me. On such a cold, wet day no sane person wore that sort of footwear.

Was this some sort of foot fetish thing? Was she going to get turned on by my hair touching her feet? And, if so, did I have enough hair to do the trick?

I sat and was enshrouded in a black cape that was tied around my throat in an instant.

'What would you like?' she asked, her long hair tickling my ears as she leaned forward to eyeball me in the mirror.

'A number three, please.'

She moved away, and started to hum as she picked up the clippers.

I looked at her feet again.

'You're not from around here, are you?' She picked up a comb.

'Nope, passing through,' I replied, averting my gaze.

We chatted about things, starting with the weather of course, then my travels and her distinct lack of interest in golf. Silence followed. She seemed so normal, I tried not to think about what she was doing with her feet. Next up was politics. Weather and politics, the staple diet of Irish conversation, usually in that order.

I was having a damn fine rant about something or other when a wasp went straight in my ear. I swore loudly and rocketed out of the chair, swatting at my ear out of reflex.

There was no wasp. The woman was shaving my ears. Dear God, she was shaving my ears. Confusion, doubt, shame – too many emotions to deal with at once. I covered my ear as if she had sliced it off. The look of shock on my face was matched by her own. She was still bent over with the clippers in the exact place where my ear had been.

'What are you doing?' I yelped.

'Tidying up your ear hair.'

Ear hair! No, no, no. For forty years my ears had lain

undisturbed, apart from the occasional cotton bud, and now they'd sprouted enough hair to be worthy of shaving. My mid-life crisis that I had regarded as being long in my future hit me like a freight train. I slid a finger into my ear . . . and felt stubble. My knees went weak and I sank back into the chair defeated. Is this what they did in Monaghan hairdressers? Were clippers about to be shoved up my nostrils?

The woman looked terrified. She apologised non-stop and looked around as if in search of glue to repair each follicle. After an awkward silence, she coughed and asked the question I knew was coming: 'Should I do the other one? You know, even things up.'

I could do nothing but nod.

You Better, You Better, You Bet

'They say golf is like life, but don't believe them. Golf is more complicated than that.'

GARDNER DICKINSON

Christmas came and went. I had seen precious little of my wife, and curling up in front of a log fire with warm dogs at my feet was a luxury that lasted beyond the heavy frosts of January.

I recall my dad's parents with huge affection and always looked forward to going down to Greystones for Sunday lunch and Gran's cooking. After lunch, I'd go to the workshop where Granddad had something he was tinkering over. He'd be making a boat for the pond that was a central part of their garden, or he'd ask Dad for help with something for the vegetable patch. He was ingenious and he had big hands that were wonderful to watch as he crafted the smallest of things.

One day he and Dad wore big smiles as they presented me with my first set of cut-down golf clubs. There were no spare putters so I was given a long tube of white plastic insulation pipe with a block of wood attached at the end. I was six years old and I loved it. That was the start of my passion for golf.

It is easy to become addicted to golf and it is a game of idiosyncrasies. No two golf swings are the same, just as no two golfers are the same. I have played alongside people who had swings you couldn't make up, let alone duplicate. From windmills to axe murderers to salsa dancers, everyone has their own style. I was lucky enough to be taught by my father and grandfather . . . and Granddad's band of cronies.

During the early years I didn't get to play with my dad very often. He worked hard in the coal mines, fifteen hours a day, toiling to put bread and milk on the table. Actually, he was a banker, and an amazing father, but he wasn't home during the week and on Saturdays he played the weekly competition at Greystones – a day juniors feared.

My grandfather, Jack, was a big man. Not quite six feet tall, he had a barrel for a chest, slick silver hair and a salt-and-pepper moustache. A big heart too. He took me out onto Greystones golf course many times over the years, slipping through a friend's garden to sneak on to the 3rd hole. There we would meet up with his gang of six brothers-in-arms and Bob. Bob was undoubtedly the canniest of the group and had a nose for finding golf balls. Charlie would turn to Bob every few holes and say 'Fetch a ball, Bob' and off Bob would lollop, reappearing only when he had a ball in his mouth. Bob was a Golden Labrador of supreme talent.

I can only remember Charlie's and Eugene's names – and Bob's, obviously. This was back in the 1970s and half of the men smoked pipes, a couple wore plus fours and flat caps were the fashion. They only played nine holes as the 'inner' nine were too hilly for them, but as a small kid that made no difference to me. Each of them had some gift to give me. Eugene was the most brilliant putter I have ever seen – and that stands to this day. He sank long-range putts frequently and inside ten feet he rarely missed. He gave me hints on how to lag a putt and read a line . . . gifts I lost long ago. Charlie was a magician around the greens, bumping an 8 iron to a couple of feet from anywhere. One of the others, a tall, willowy figure who always looked under-nourished, tried to show me how to hit the low punch shot, while my granddad was all power with that big chest of his.

'Don't worry about where it goes,' he used to say. 'Hit it long and we'll fine-tune the direction later.'

That was easy to say when I was eight or nine years old because the ball went only a hundred yards or so. My direction is little better today, but the ball goes 250 yards and there's a lot more damage a ball can do at that distance.

Perhaps it was those special memories that made me keen to keep my baseball grip. I didn't like the more widely-used interlocking grip and, after I and several kids went to Bray Golf Club to get lessons from the club Pro, I was more determined than ever to stick with what I knew.

'No, don't grip it like that,' the Pro said immediately, yanking the club out of my hand. 'Like this.'

He hadn't let me hit a ball. I was eleven and I was damn good, demonstrating a modesty few eleven-year-olds can achieve.

'But . . .' I started.

'Like this,' he repeated, shoving his interlocking grip into my face.

'My granddad showed me . . .'

'Well, he's wrong.' He checked that I was holding the club the way he wanted me to and then signalled for me to hit the ball.

I hit three shots, none of which went more than five yards.

'Next,' he yelled.

It was because of that experience that I felt so much empathy for the kid at Enniscorthy Golf Club. He was in his teens, gangly and clearly confused. He was standing on the 1st tee with an older man who was doling out advice.

'Put your hands like that,' the man said, demonstrating the baseball grip on the club he held.

'Like this?' the kid asked, using the reverse grip favoured by hurlers.

'No, the other way around.'

'That's mad, I can't do that.'

'Try.'

'No.'

'Go on, would you? There are people waiting.' The exasperation in the man's voice was obvious as he glanced behind and nodded an apology to the waiting group.

The kid tried it, complained some more and finally heaved the big shoulder-shrugging sigh perfected by teenagers the world over.

'Now what?' he asked.

'Now hit the ball.'

The kid looked dubious, took a swing and scuffed the ball two feet. 'Jeez, this is a stupid game,' he muttered. 'Can I try it my way now?'

The man gave him a ball. The kid dropped it on the ground, ignoring the wooden tee, reversed his hands into a cack-handed grip and ripped his tee shot straight down the fairway.

Sometimes there's natural talent . . . and sometimes we have to work hard to get to where we want to be. Most golfers I know are scared of taking golf lessons, terrified by the consequences of change. All those fears that flood in: will he alter my grip? Will he ruin the one strong part of my game? Will he laugh and shout 'Next'?

It took me twenty years before I attempted a lesson again and Karl, the Greystones Pro, gave me enough advice that saw me drop from double figures to a single figure handicap in a year.

At the end of the lessons he said: 'Now we've got those little things sorted out we can start working on the serious problems.'

'Next!' I shouted and fled.

The guys I met at Mount Wolseley introduced me to a completely new world of competitive golf.

'You OK with five, five and five?' Niall asked as we shook hands on the 1st tee. He was a big lad in his thirties, casually dressed and had hands the size of dinner plates. Judging by his girth he liked to eat, so I fancied my chances. The only issue was Mount Wolseley itself. We were playing in an Open Competition, on a course designed by Christy O'Connor Junior. That meant it would be long and tough. We were going to be out there for five hours plus.

'Sure,' I said. 'Why not?'

'The four behind us are in on the bet as well,' Niall said. 'We play a lot of these things together.'

Dave stepped forward at that point. 'Be fair, Niall.' He turned to me. 'When he says five, five and five he means five hundred, five hundred, five hundred.'

'As in Euro?' I squeaked.

'As in Euro, yes.'

'Fifteen hundred quid a man?' I was shocked. 'Are you solicitors or something?'

Dave laughed. 'Hell no. Niall and Ian are carpenters, I'm a plasterer. Same for the guys behind, but Jimmy's a developer.'

The Celtic Tiger was roaring at the time and these guys were the living proof. In such demand, they could charge what they liked and then throw it about on the golf course as if it was confetti. I declined to join their match and discovered some interesting additional twists along the way.

We were on the 5th hole, a par five, and Niall had reached the green in two. Rotund he may have been but he hit the ball a mile. His putt snaked across the surface and dropped into the hole for an eagle. There were whoops of delight while the other two shook their heads despondently.

'What?' I asked Dave.

'If you get an eagle, everyone else has to pay you €250. He's just made €1,500.' Dave was none too pleased. 'He did it last week as well.'

Their rules were simple: a birdie meant everyone else paid you €50, an eagle got you €250, while a double bogey resulted in a forfeit of €100. It was an expensive business.

'It is expensive, sure,' Niall said later, 'but overall everything evens out over a number of matches.'

Except when they lure in mugs like me who would never have the chance to win it back. I had enjoyed the day, and the course, but sitting in the bar afterwards, as large sums of cash were passed around, I calculated how much I would have lost if I'd joined their pot. One eagle and five birdies would have cost me €500, but it was my two double bogeys that would have been the most punitive, costing me a mere €1,400. Add on the initial bet and I would have forked out €3,400.

I might as well have given them the keys to Rusty . . . and I'd still have needed a visit to the bank.

I genuinely like a flutter on a game, but anything more than a few Euro and it can get stressful. It can also make your playing partners too aggressive, cheering your missed putts as happened to me once . . . and that stops it being enjoyable.

I was heading northeast, enjoying the lush Gowran Park, the classic Carlow and the sheep-strewn fairways of The Curragh along the way. The River Barrow was a constant companion, its velvet waters gliding beside the road that took me from Carlow town to Athy. It is the second-longest river in Ireland, rising in the Slieve Bloom Mountains, where I would be in the weeks ahead, and finding its way to meet the ocean in Waterford. I was following its route into the midlands of Ireland and I hadn't been paying attention.

It was late February and the centre of the country was bitterly cold – and would remain so right through spring. 'Cold' in the midlands means one thing: frost.

Winter frost looks beautiful, layered over the ground like a sheet and creating mesmerising patterns on the windscreen. It crunches underfoot and turns breath into billowing clouds that drift through the air. Frost also closes golf courses and, while the crunchy-underfoot-breath-billowing thing is all fine and dandy, it's of little consolation when you're still sitting in the camper van at 11 a.m. and your tee time was 7.30 a.m.

My trip to Newbridge Golf Club drove this home in more ways than one. I arrived at the club late one evening, with not a vehicle in the car park and the clubhouse black and impenetrable.

I parked near the clubhouse and opened the fridge door in the hope that something delicious had appeared miraculously during the day. As on so many occasions, I was left disappointed. A quick rifle through the cupboard revealed my choices were pasta or pasta. I picked the pasta only to find that the gas hob didn't want to know. It had always required a bit of work and a gentle touch, but tonight it refused to ignite. I felt a sense of dread as I turned to the gas heater. No dice there, either.

Not good. I stepped out of the camper van and checked the gas tank. It was empty, which meant no heat. Definitely not good. It was bitterly cold and I'd heard the word 'freezing' being tossed about in The Curragh clubhouse. It was early enough so I drove back in to Newbridge, across the railway tracks and proceeded to visit every petrol station around the town – six of them – as well as Woodies DIY. They had plenty of gas cylinders, but not the propane one that I needed. It was going to be a cold night.

'Take a hot water bottle,' my wife had said while I was packing Rusty the week before. 'You never know.'

Wise words and thankfully I had paid attention. On the way back to the club I stopped at one of the petrol stations and filled up the hot water bottle at the coffee station, receiving odd looks from the late night shoppers.

To show willing, I bought a chocolate bar.

The young man behind the counter looked at me as he zapped the bar. 'Anything else?'

'No,' I replied.

'That wasn't coffee you put in there, was it?'

I held up the bottle. 'Have you ever tasted coffee from a hot water bottle?'

He confessed that he hadn't.

'It's disgusting. Seriously, don't ever try it.'

He nodded and pursed his lips like he was storing away that nugget of information should such a day ever come, and charged me for the bar.

I grew up in a boarding school high on a hillside, where the powers that be believed it would build character to turn on the central heating only when it hit 0 °C, and where we slept in dorms with windows that were so old they didn't shut. We knew a thing or two about the cold.

Maybe I'd grown softer with age because I went to bed

that night wearing three pairs of socks, a beanie and half of my wardrobe on top of the duvet.

I woke up in the dark with a bad feeling. Well, it wasn't a feeling, more that I didn't have any feeling at all. I scrunched my toes, heard snapping like twigs and tried to find the hot water bottle. It was cold. As I reached for the light I took a deep breath and listened to it rattling in my lungs.

Staying in bed was pointless. It was 5 a.m., which had a nice symmetry to it as the temperature outside was -5 °C. How cold was it inside? -5 °C. The quandary I faced was how to get dressed. I mean, have you ever put on boxer shorts that are frozen stiff? My advice is, don't. It's like placing your privates in an ice bucket and adding piranhas that haven't eaten in a week. It gives new meaning to 'biting cold'.

As I staggered around trying to warm up my clothes I realised there was only one way to get any warmth into the camper van. I grabbed the generator, jumped out onto the tarmac and fired it up. I plugged in my laptop and proceeded to sit on the adaptor until the first tentacles of warmth began to seep up through my buttocks. It was bliss.

I worked on the computer for what felt like hours, shifting from one buttock to the other, until I heard the sound of a car arriving. Daylight had finally arrived and I watched the car draw up beside me.

There was a knock at the door.

'Are you alive in there?' the young man asked when I opened the door. He was encased in several layers of clothing and a coat I would have killed for.

'Come into the clubhouse,' he continued. 'We'll get you warmed up.'

Jamie was the owner's son and head greenkeeper, and while Elaine prepared coffee and toast, I told Jamie about my propane problem.

'I'll sort that out for you. I doubt there's a propane cylinder around here but I know a place in Naas.'

I was eternally grateful and we walked out to Rusty to remove the cylinder.

'Leave it by the door,' Jamie said, indicating a spot. 'I'll go and get you a full one when I've finished the course inspection.' He blew a long breath and we watched it in the air. 'You won't be playing for a while in these conditions.'

Elaine had put the grub on the table by the time I returned. I don't drink coffee, but I drank what she'd put on the table and then asked for more. Anything for a bit of warmth.

We chatted, or should I say she chatted while I stuffed myself with food and hot liquid. I stayed there for ages, abusing her hospitality as prickles of warmth spread through my body. When I returned from playing the course, Elaine was waiting for me with soup and sandwiches.

To complete my visit, a shiny new propane tank had been left beside Rusty.

It is one of the bonuses of visiting small country clubs. That family friendly atmosphere – even when it's not family – is a pleasure to experience. They can't do enough for you, they treat you like long-lost friends and make sure you leave with a smile on your face. The high-profile courses are friendly too, but they manage you in a practical, professional manner. It's why places that combine the two really stand out. The mighty European Club is run by the Ruddys, so it has that relaxed family feel, while Mount Juliet offers one of the great welcomes in Irish golf.

I wound my way across the Kildare and Laois countryside, getting closer and closer to the Slieve Bloom Mountains that crested the horizon. I played Dunmurry Springs, a new course that boasts views of seven counties from its highest point, before arriving at The Heritage at Killenard, designed by Seve Ballesteros. The hotel and clubhouse are spectacular creations, but they are cramped by all the housing that has been built around them. It's the curse of modern golf development: build a golf course and then build the houses that will help pay for it.

I was involved with the marketing before the course opened in 2004, writing brochures, advertisements and a radio ad for the great man himself. The Director of Golf took me out in a 4x4 and we drove around the course, with the greens only sand plateaus and the fairways in their infancy.

Perhaps I was expecting too much; perhaps I was anticipating that, after all my efforts to promote the resort, the place owed me. It didn't.

Bad golf always comes out of the blue and, unlike good golf, it always hangs on, dragging you down in spirit and energy. That is the worst part of this game because it feels like a dead weight that threatens to drown you.

At The Heritage, my bad golf started on the 1st tee and never let up. A wild swing sent the ball almost into the houses. I never found it, nor did I find the provisional that followed the first. I managed a repeat on the 2nd and again on the 8th. By the back nine I was sinking fast, water now attracting my ball like a magnet. Why I was making such a balls-up, I don't know, but the *coup de grâce* came on the 18th, when I lightened my bag by another two balls. Eight lost balls . . . at least. I tried everything but the more I tried, the worse it got. If you're a golfer you'll know exactly what I mean. My pride and self-belief were battered as I limped off the final green.

Maybe I ate in the clubhouse; maybe I didn't. I don't remember. There's nothing quite like the despair of golf. It can rip away at your soul because you have too much time to think and analyse everything as you trudge towards your next shot. And the one after that . . .

I read a golf psychology book once, many years ago. It said that I should focus on the shot to come and erase the bad shots from my memory. I tried hard to cast aside those many shots I played at The Heritage, but when I looked back down the fairway, there they were, following me in an orderly queue. 'Hi,' they said in unison, 'remember us.' I smiled, nodded, took a swing and the queue grew.

The Heath Golf Club, no more than twenty minutes' drive down the road, did not provide the bounce I desired. Just the opposite, as reflected by the twenty-one points on my scorecard. Despite its ocean of yellow gorse sweeping around the course, my dark cloud of gloom only deepened. After arriving with such a burst the previous day the cloud was determined to linger, sapping my confidence. I started to reach that horrible place all golfers try so hard to avoid.

'Why do I play this game? I don't enjoy it. I should pack it in and take up knitting.'

I couldn't see a way out of it and that was the scariest thing of all. In less than twenty-four hours I had been reduced to an inept idiot, spraying drives nationwide and cramming so many negative thoughts into my swing I was lucky to hit the ball.

There are people who play golf to take the stress out of life, and there are people who play golf and get stressed. Sometimes, it's hard to believe that this is supposed to be fun.

That night I sat in the camper van and looked at the list of all the courses I had played and what was to come. I wasn't yet halfway through my list and my enthusiasm was waning fast. It was cold, courses were closed from the frost, it got dark at 5 p.m. and I was stuck alone in car parks at night because clubhouses were closed. This was a stupid idea, I decided. Dumb. Idiotic. It was time to go home and get back to the real world.

I called my wife and laid it all out. I told her I was coming home.

'Oh, stop being such a drama queen and get on with it,' she said.

Yes dear.

I walked into Portarlington's clubhouse that same night thinking I'd get drunk and drown my negative feelings that way. It would impair my golf the following morning but at least I'd have an excuse.

I was sitting opposite the entrance to the lounge when a man pushed through the doors and looked around. He smiled at the barman.

'That was better than The K Club!' he announced loudly, although I couldn't see his lips move through the bushy goatee that must have been removed from a Brillo pad packet that morning. It was quite resplendent. The remains of how many previous meals it contained was anyone's guess.

It was an outrageous statement and it grabbed everyone's attention. He looked my way and gave me a wink. 'Now, where's my free pint?'

He didn't get his free pint but I was tempted to give him the full glass I had on the table. The K Club is one of Ireland's top courses, with thirty-six holes and the Ryder Cup to its name. It's a venue everybody knows; Portarlington not so much. If he was serious, then I didn't want to be playing with a hangover the following morning and he was welcome to my pint. Finally, something to lift my spirits.

So did the day when I strode out to the 1st tee at daybreak. It was calm and sunny. The wildlife was out and about, tracks meandering through glistening dew, across fairways and greens. There was no sign of frost and the course was glorious. Those dark clouds hanging over me evaporated in a cartoon-like puff.

Portarlington is no K Club, but that made it no less exciting. What country golf club could compete with the manicured nirvana and pretentiousness of The K Club? What country club would want to? Portarlington is flat and it weaves between tall, mature trees and beside the River Barrow that slinks its way alongside a few holes. It is gentle and idyllic and I had more fun than I'd had in a long time. The golf wasn't that good, but it wasn't appalling either.

Nearby, off the M7 motorway, was the small town of Mountrath, which was once renowned for its endless rush hour traffic jams, thanks to a 90-degree-bend in the town centre. The motorway has done away with those, and I drove around that feared corner with not another car in sight. I passed Tom Delaney's pub, where friends and I often pulled in to avoid those traffic jams. Three of us once decided to jump out and walk the few hundred yards to town, past the stationary traffic. We left Mark to drive the remaining distance and join us in the pub, but he never showed. An hour later, a couple of pints to the good, we headed outside to find Mark pulling in to a parking spot. He wasn't impressed when we jumped in and told him thanks very much, now let's get going.

Mountrath Golf Club, where I was headed, is farther out of town on the way to Borris-in-Ossory.

As part of my economy/health drive, I ate many of my meals in the camper van. A two-ringed gas hob was the extent of the cooking facilities, which, for my culinary prowess, was more than enough. At one stage I tried making porridge. It didn't work out too well, but at least a local builder offered to take it away for use as cement. It took me three days to chisel the porridge off the saucepan. Cooking dinner proved an even bigger challenge. I called my wife and asked for instructions.

'Boil the water,' she said patiently. 'Is it boiling yet?'

'Yes.'

'Now put the egg in the water for three minutes.'

'How?'

She hung up.

It turns out that there are easier things to prepare than a boiled egg. Pasta is as easy as it comes. The hardest part is opening the bag and not spraying the contents everywhere. I stretched my abilities by introducing different types. There was spaghetti, fusilli, tagliatelle, rigatoni and farfalloni. At times I thought I was cooking the Italian football team. I ate a lot of pasta on my travels and that night at Mountrath, it was penne.

I stirred the pot, the pasta sauce slowly coagulating at the bottom.

'Ah go on, would you?' I muttered at the reluctant foodstuff.

Through the open window I could see the clubhouse lights and people moving back and forth, laughing, drinking and eating. How I envied them. I stirred some more. The popular brand of sauce I used came in varieties such as yellow pepper, chorizo and mixed vegetable. I had renamed them to more closely match their true flavours, and tonight's meal was chorizo chunder.

Wafts of seriously tasty cooking drifted on the breeze . . . and then came the smell of bacon. I have vegetarian friends who get starry-eyed at the smell and stumble about frothing at the mouth. I gritted my teeth and stirred some more. My wooden spoon was struggling to navigate the sludge of red gunge that called itself food. When all you have to do is pour a pot of sauce into one pan, and boil some pasta in another, it's as simple a meal as you can ask for. It's difficult to screw up but I still managed.

Tonight was worse than usual. The sludge of sauce was going nowhere. A minute later I looked more closely.

'Bollocks,' I said. I hadn't turned on the gas.

I tossed it in the bin and stomped off to the clubhouse.

'Burger,' I said, 'with extra bacon.'

It's no surprise that golf clubs stick to a relatively short and identical menu. Slap on a burger, a lasagne, a chicken curry, a sandwich and the full Irish and you've satisfied 95 per cent of the golfing population. There's always someone who wants something green on their plate, but they're usually ignored or given mushy peas. I ate some delicious food – Seapoint's chicken stir-fry was evidence of an adventurous chef who hadn't yet grasped the golf food concept – and I ate food that hurt. The burger at Thurles should have been seconded by the gardaí to batter the Shell protesters, while the cheese on Mallow's lasagne proved an excellent way to seal Rusty's roof.

The burger at Mountrath was very good and the bacon perfectly crisp. The mushy peas I left.

The Slieve Bloom Mountains, the oldest mountains in Europe, were to the north as I travelled to Roscrea, along the old main road. For once I needed no maps to find the golf course as the entrance was clearly marked on the main road. I still went sailing by, shocked to have found it so easily.

Roscrea Golf Club has been around since 1892, but a refurbishment of the clubhouse means it has the best-looking bar in the country. It's an elegant horseshoe of dark wood that lends itself to high stools, long chats and everyone sticking their oar in. As I nestled up and ordered a pint I glanced out at the rain that had started an hour earlier, and wondered how Rusty was going to hold up.

There were three lads sitting at the bar, discussing the weather. Simply by being there I was drawn into the conversation.

'The weather's terrible, terrible, isn't it?' asked the oldest of the group, turning to me. His gnarly fingers were hooked around a glass of hot whiskey, a waft of steam rising in a lazy spiral. His hands, huge and weather-beaten, made the glass look about the size of a thimble. 'No one's going to go out in that.' He gestured towards the window where the rain rattled against the glass so hard it was practically vibrating.

I nodded in agreement.

'Weather forecasters got it wrong again,' said another.

I shook my head and shrugged at the injustice of it all.

'Soft day my arse,' the final man growled into his glass. 'Wouldn't know a soft day if it walked up and bit them.'

The second one eyed me from head to toe. 'Are you waiting to go out and play?'

'I've come a long way,' I replied.

He sucked air in through his teeth. 'You should have picked a better day.'

We talked long about the weather. It's a national pastime after all, and still the rain fell.

The next day was dry, but I thought nothing of the damp patch under the front of the camper van. I assumed it was run-off water from the night before. My mistake.

I drove around Roscrea town and headed north for Birr on the N62, the Slieve Blooms now to my east. It was as I approached the village of Sharavogue that I noticed the temperature gauge rising.

'That can't be good,' I muttered. I then used all of my technical expertise, gleaned over many years, and tapped at the gauge.

I frowned when nothing happened because that nearly

always worked. There was a picnic area ahead so I pulled in. It was a beauty spot, with views cascading across to the mountains, but my thoughts were elsewhere. I tapped at the gauge again, watching as it stayed resolutely in the red section.

I removed the bonnet and stared vacantly into the interior.

I know my way around an engine as well as a badger knows its way around a black tie ball: I think I know what I'm looking at but I couldn't be more wrong.

None the wiser, I got back behind the wheel and drove on to Birr, albeit slowly. It never occurred to me that it was the water tank. If it had and I'd tackled the problem in time it would have saved me a lot of money and my wife a lot of grief.

With the gauge remaining firmly in the red I stayed overnight at Birr Golf Club, and departed the following morning in the hope that everything had miraculously fixed itself. I had gone only a few miles towards Athlone when the gauge started rising. I turned Rusty around and we limped our way back into Birr town. I parked on the outskirts and addressed what needed to be done next. It didn't help that it was a Sunday and 99 per cent of businesses close on a Sunday in the country. I called my insurance company and they said nothing would happen until Monday and to call back then. Thanks a bunch. I walked into town, found Dooly's Hotel serving breakfast and was extremely pleasant to the receptionist, an older woman by the name of Valerie. With her hair tied in a bun and her glasses perched on her nose, she had a matronly look. I explained my problems.

She slapped her hands on the desk and leapt from the chair. Valerie picked up her phone and snapped out instructions. She was the sort of front-of-house woman you need at a hotel. Within minutes I had four members of staff, all dressed in their black waistcoats, at my beck and call. I repeated my troubles and they rushed off in different directions while I stood there and marvelled.

'OK,' Brian said, somewhat out of breath. He was the first to return and Valerie gave me a nod to indicate that Brian was her star recruit. 'I have some names here who might be able to help.'

He was a portly young guy, in his twenties, with a roundish, happy face. Topped off with light curly hair he had that slightly teddy bear look. You couldn't but like the guy.

He handed me a piece of paper and pointed out the names.

'Mick's your best bet. He's local and a good mechanic. Can fix anything. But don't get him talking or you'll never hear the end of it.' He pointed at the next name. 'Shay's out Sharavogue way and has his own pit. You'll have to get someone to tow you out there though.'

The other three recruits had returned by this point, all bearing their gifts of names, telephone numbers and instructions. I was talked through each one, with Mick's number appearing on all four pieces. I'd be calling Mick, so.

I thanked them profusely. It had been a rescue mission and for the moment I felt rescued. I went and ate breakfast, taking my time. With kids, Mass and Sunday lunch it was pointless phoning anyone before the afternoon.

On my way out I walked over to Valerie to thank her again for the help and hospitality that the Irish are renowned for.

'I'd let you make calls from here but I can't tie up the phone,' she explained.

I glanced at the old black phone, admiring the long handset cord that spiralled to the floor and curled itself into a giant heap beside the desk. It looked like she could walk anywhere in the hotel and still be on the phone, although Health & Safety might have something to say about that.

'I'm sorry to say that Birr Castle is closed at the moment. It would have been lovely for you to see it.' She reached over to a bank of tourist leaflets and removed one. 'Here,' she said, 'so you can see what you're missing.'

I stepped out onto the Square and tried to decide which way to go. The town's Georgian character was everywhere I looked. It has retained its wide streets and its Georgian buildings, and I wandered along quite surprised at what I was seeing. Birr is designated as an Irish Heritage Town and it's easy to see why. By chance I walked along Green Street, making straight for the castellated wall that marked Birr Castle Demesne and the 100 acres of castle and grounds that lie beyond. The castle, which dates back to 1170, was home to the appropriately named Leviathan, the largest telescope in the world for many years in the 1800s. Following the death of the man who built it – the 3rd Earl of Rosse – and that of his son, the telescope fell into disrepair and was eventually melted down to help with the First World War efforts. The telescope was restored to its former glory in the 1990s.

I continued my circuit, marching alongside the grey, stone walls of Rosse Row, until I reached Oxmantown Mall. The name caught my interest and I turned down a street with mature trees lining the right and a terrace of Georgian houses opposite. The front doors were brightly coloured and topped with fan lights. Combined with the sash windows, Wisteria and Virginia Creeper climbing the walls, it was utterly charming. I would have enjoyed it a lot more if it hadn't started raining.

This was real Irish rain. None of that 'soft rain' malarkey that was invented by Bord Fáilte. I understand why they did it. Attracting tourists to Ireland has always been cursed by the prospect of non-stop rain . . . big thundering bullets of water pounding down so hard that they bounce up as high as your knees.

Bord Fáilte had a brainstorming session to identify how they could weaken this myth that it always rained in Ireland. They couldn't change the facts so they changed the terminology, and 'soft rain' got the government stamp of approval. Under the little known Rain Act of 1970, all government departments, semi-state bodies and public organisations were, in the interests of tourism, to refer to all types of rain as 'soft'. It even sounds cuddly or like something you'd have as a side dish in a fancy restaurant: I'll have Terrine of Suckling Pig, Warm Brioche, Autumn Greens and Soft Rain.

What was coming out of the sky in Birr was far from cuddly. It hurt. I ran as fast as I could for as long as I could, reaching the other side of the street before the exhaustion turned me into a heaving wreck. Golfers aren't designed for speed.

It was a long, wet walk back to Rusty.

I sat at the camper van table with a saucepan beside me collecting the water leaking through the roof. It wasn't even a drip anymore: this was a full scale Gwyneth Paltrow acceptance speech. Every fifteen minutes I had to lean over and empty the saucepan down the sink, holding a towel over my head to stop myself getting wet. The generator was running outside, tucked underneath the camper, so I could work. Not that it was proving productive. Between the dripping water, the saucepan emptying and two kids who decided banging on the side of the camper van every two minutes was a hilarious thing to do, I spent most of the time crying.

At 3 p.m. I started making calls to the numbers I had been given. As Valerie had indicated, getting through on a

Sunday was impossible. Mick's number, Shay's number and all the other numbers I had been given rang and rang. I tried several times until finally there was a click and the automated female voicemail response kicked in:

'We're sorry, the number you are calling is not available at the moment. Please try again later and please stop annoying people on a Sunday. Wait until tomorrow like everybody else.'

And I did.

By 9.30 on Monday morning, Eugene King was head down under the bonnet. I'd called the insurance company at 9 a.m. and they'd called Eugene. He had the problem identified in moments, but it was of little help.

'It's a cracked water tank,' he said, 'and that's not something you can fix on the side of the road. You need to get to a garage.'

After a brief discussion he started making calls. He was a trim man in his late fifties and he didn't muck about. After the fifth or sixth call he hung up.

'I'll take you to the garage up the road,' he said. 'They can sort you out.'

I followed him along Birr's streets to Syngefield. He introduced me to Michael and then said his goodbyes.

Michael was the service manager. His snappy suit gave him more of a salesman look, but he sat me down in the waiting room and went off to find a mechanic.

He came back with two and I watched as they clambered underneath Rusty, peered into the engine and scratched their heads.

'Yea,' I muttered to myself, 'I tried that too.'

After a conference on the forecourt, Michael returned.

'I'm afraid it's going to cost you if you want us to do it here,' he said, matter-of-factly. 'We'll have to put her in a pit to remove and replace the water tank. It's very tight in there. To be honest, the lads aren't sure they might not do other damage. There are lots of wires and lines that could get broken.'

I appreciated his honesty. During the drive up to the garage behind Eugene, I had watched as the temperature gauge began its inexorable rise towards the red, crushing my optimism that Rusty might magically have fixed itself overnight. I knew I had no choice if I wanted to get back on the road and back to smashing a ball.

'How much?' I asked.

'Fifteen hundred,' he replied.

A week later, after my wife had driven from Wexford to Birr to peel my still-speechless body off the waiting room floor, we made the two-and-a-half-hour return journey. I paid out the €1,500, loaded up the camper van and said goodbye to my wife. As she headed home, I headed north to Athlone.

This is the centre of the country, on the border between counties Roscommon and Westmeath. The town is famous for many things, including being home to the oldest pub in Ireland. It's a small spit-and-sawdust place called Sean's Bar, and it dates back to the tenth century. My original itinerary had included a visit to Sean's, with its low ceilings, dark wood and walls covered in photographs, posters and other paraphernalia, but that was before Rusty's breakdown and the enormous dent in my wallet. I had a schedule to catch up on and Sean's Bar would have to be sacrificed.

The town is split almost in half by the River Shannon, and, as I crossed the bridge to reach my next destination, I left Westmeath and entered County Roscommon.

As I played Athlone Golf Club a couple of miles outside the town, I was enjoying the sunshine and the club's location on the shores of Lough Ree. I was on the 3rd hole when I noticed the ominous clouds heading my way. They were as black as anything I'd seen, thin fingers stretching ahead of the mass, almost as a warning. I was still bathed in sunshine, but not for much longer. I pulled on my waterproofs and looked across at Rusty in the distance. I hadn't left any pots on the floor.

The rain hit as I drove off the 399-metre 4th. The wind followed in a brutal arc that switched from vertical to horizontal in seconds. I leaned into it, first with my head, then my shoulders, then my entire body until my nose was sliding between blades of grass. It was a transformation of 249 metres. I know this because my nose grazed the 150-metre fairway marker.

The wind still managed to drive sleet into my face. I had two hats on but my hands were turning numb. I made no attempt to play my ball, either on the 4th or 5th holes. It was a downpour of misery. Yet, by the time I reached the 6th, the rain had been replaced by sunshine.

Perhaps what is most interesting about the stereotypical view of Irish rain is that it doesn't rain as much as you'd think . . . good news for Bord Fáilte. The Irish Meteorological Service keeps an eye on such things, and their figures show that if you took all the time that it rains in a year and added it together, it comes to fifty days of rain. Which means that it doesn't rain on the other 315 days.

If you're hunched under an umbrella as the rain pounds down, and you've discovered that your waterproofs aren't actually waterproof, I appreciate that these statistics are scant consolation. My point is you mustn't assume that because you are in Ireland you're going to endure rain – be it soft rain or any other variety. In Tom Coyne's book, *A Course Called Ireland*, he played all the island's links in what appeared to be a single, non-stop torrential downpour. I played those same links and, apart from a lengthy delay at Rosses Point, I was rained on not once.

The offer I had received from Glasson could not have been timed better. My wet clothes and shoes were stinking up the joint and a night away from Rusty would give everything a chance to mellow. Glasson Golf Resort sits on the opposite shore of Lough Ree to Athlone, and comes with a hotel on the slopes above the lake. Gareth, the resort's manager, offered me a room and I accepted. And some room it was. It was practically a suite, with a fireplace and a pair of sofas facing each other, well away from the bed. It had views of the golf course and the lough.

It was easy to see I was getting the special treatment. Not so, I discovered.

'All our rooms are exactly the same,' Gareth informed me the following day.

I have never stayed in a hotel so focused on golfers, not even the new hotel at Carnoustie. I could see why Glasson was a popular base from which to explore the surrounding golf clubs.

The road was taking me east, through a midlands littered with golf courses. Attractive ones, odd ones, old ones and new ones. Mount Temple has ceramic rabbits on its tee boxes. The further your round progresses the fewer body parts these rabbits have as golfers vent their frustrations or their sadistic nature. By the 15th they've demonstrated impressive survival instincts and migrated to the ladies' tees. Mullingar boasts the friendliest welcome in Ireland . . . and they're spot on. It is also one of the great and distinguished inland courses. Kilcock has been remodelled and re-greened, after buying and shifting the greens from the defunct old Dun Laoghaire and Bray golf courses. Who says Ireland doesn't recycle.

'You know how golf works, don't you?'

I was standing in the car park at Kilcock when their manager popped the strangest question I had been asked on my travels.

'How do you mean?'

'Well, for instance, do you know what bogeys and birdies are?'

'Yes,' I replied hesitantly, thinking there was a joke coming.

'You do? Oh good. Off you go then,' he said pointing to the 1st tee. 'I thought I was going to have to explain it to you.'

He headed back to his office, leaving me perplexed. Why would I be writing a book about golf if I didn't know how the game was played?

That said, one time I was at a party in London and met a guy – he called himself a poet – who boasted that he had written a travel book on Australia, but had never been.

When I asked him how he did it, he tossed his head back and laughed in the way poets do.

'I contacted the Australian embassy and asked them to send me all their travel books. Then I chose the bits I wanted and put them altogether.'

Hopefully his plagiarism was better than his poetry, which we had to endure for much of the night. It was a combination of alliteration and rap.

As someone pointed out at the end of the night, the reason it's called rap is because the 'c' fell off.

I played the gentle parkland of Kilcock, finding myself going back and forth with plenty of bogeys but no birdies, before leaving County Meath for County Kildare.

My arrival at Moyvalley Golf Club on the Kildare border introduced me to the full excesses of the Celtic Tiger economy. Designed by Darren Clarke and with a joining fee of €75,000, it came with the ubiquitous hotel and housing.

It was opened to huge fanfare in 2006, and has struggled ever since.

The clubhouse and vast car park were bathed in sunshine, yet there were only three cars on the tarmac. Inside, the clubhouse wasn't quite as lively as a funeral parlour. For a glamour resort such as this to be so dead on a Saturday was a startling sight. I was due to play the following morning, but with no other golfer in sight I asked Tristan, the club Pro, if I could play that afternoon.

Fifteen minutes later I was on the 1st tee. It wasn't until the 17th that I saw another golfer.

The problem Moyvalley encountered was that locals wouldn't and couldn't pay a €75,000 joining fee. It was the highest fee at the time and, with Dublin almost an hour away, the rich bankers and developers who were propping up the economy on empty promises had other glamour resorts to choose from, such as Carton House and The K Club. It was practically born to fail.

It's a shame, too, because I liked Moyvalley: its sweet, lazy rhythm of rolling fairways and pristine greens is almost soporific.

Rusty wasn't always welcome in car parks. Security was their concern, they said, which I interpreted as 'we don't want that eyesore here where our members/guests might see it and think this is a downmarket club'. Tristan had no problem with me parking overnight at the golf club, but he told me it shut at 6 p.m. He suggested I drive over to the hotel for some food and drink. It was the hotel that didn't want me in their car park.

A man in a black suit, wearing a badge that claimed his name was 'Kevin', pointed me down towards the housing estate when I asked about staying.

'Please park down there where our guests can't see you.'

Not impressed by his tone, I drove into the housing estate that surrounds the hotel to discover it was still a building site. Rubble, metal bars, piles of bricks and a couple of hard hats provided an obstacle course as I found a spot out of sight of the hotel. At least the street lighting was working so I could walk to and from the hotel without tripping over and breaking my neck.

When I pulled back the curtains the next morning the world had turned white. I opened the door thinking it had snowed, but the ground, the houses, the trees and anything I could see were drenched in hoar frost. The air was still and silent, and a thin mist was suspended on puppet strings above the houses. Even my breath hung in the dead air as if someone had hit the pause button. I had never seen anything like it but one thing was for sure: I was delighted I'd played Moyvalley the day before because no golf course was going to open in these conditions.

Nothing happened for over three hours. The world had simply stopped, the play button forgotten. The fernlike ice crystals that spread across the windscreen like a tapestry were beautiful in their complexity. I regretted having to turn the windscreen wipers on, but I had somewhere to be. I drove by the hotel and then out towards the golf course and the elegant Balyna House that used to be the focal point of this large Kildare estate. The road hugs the 10th hole and as I passed the large oak, standing alone on the fairway and wearing its white cloak of ice, a beam of sunlight pierced the mists and lit up the tree.

Less than fifteen minutes away, but in another county, is a golf course I fell deeply in love with. I drove down country lanes, watching the frost evaporate as the sun played its hand, filtering through the trees overhead and turning the white road back to black. I still had to wait a while before playing

Rathcore Golf Club, but I would have waited a lot longer to play this beauty. Family-owned and spread over a tumbling, gorse-covered landscape, Rathcore was the sort of place I had been looking for. New, like Moyvalley, it had smaller aspirations than its neighbour.

Rathcore was the brainchild of Mick and Austin Lyons, well-known Meath GAA players who had the foresight to bring in Irish course designer Mel Flanagan. I played on my own once the course opened and had plenty of time to dwell on what had been created here. I was in awe of a hidden gem that remains hidden to this day.

On my way home I visited two major resorts: the mighty Carton House and the grandiose K Club, where I have played a few times over the years, most notably at my great mate Finbarr's stag party in 1999. The rain came down so hard that day it sprayed us through our umbrellas. Back then only the Palmer course was open. I don't like the green fees or the pretentiousness of The K Club, but the Palmer course is a superb Irish experience (Smurfit I like a lot less). I emphasise 'Irish' because before the Ryder Cup in 2006, Bruce Selcraig, an American golf writer, visited and wrote a scathing review pointing out that in the US, K-Club-type courses were practically the norm.

One quote includes the following choice passage:

'Seriously. Was there not some adult in charge when the decision was made that Ireland's first Ryder Cup, a monumental event that will forever imprint Irish golf upon the world's frontal lobe, would be played at the World Headquarters of Boring, Pretentious Golf?'

He also made a reference to all the Mercedes being driven around the place. Not surprisingly, The K Club wasn't best pleased and hit back. But instead of addressing the criticisms, they responded in the manner of a petulant child, saying that if it was only Mercedes in the car park then it must have been Ladies' Day, as it was usually Porsches and Bentleys.

Here's my foot, here's my mouth. Please insert.

Superiority is one thing; smug arrogance another entirely.

You won't find such an attitude at the more down-to-earth courses that followed my K Club visit. Naas, Killeen, Craddockstown, Castlewarden and Beech Park took me back towards Dublin along the M7 motorway. Good, unassuming courses, they were packed with local golfers who are the lifeblood of Irish golf.

The M7 links up with Dublin's notorious M50, so named because it is twice as bad as London's M25. Actually, that is neither fair nor true. The M50 has been vastly improved in recent years and I sped around it to get to a small, golf-course-infested piece of north Dublin surrounding Donabate. Two of the courses are links, and what different links they are: the municipal, tight and friendly Corballis; and the big and brilliant The Island.

I had been playing a lot of golf, two rounds a day most days, and by the time I'd played Beaverstown, Balcarrick and Donabate, the joint I'd sprained on my right foot at Rosapenna was swollen and causing problems.

'Is it OK if I walk the course?' I asked the young guy in the Corballis shop. The clubhouse was basic at best, but for a €20 green fee you can't really complain.

'Sure.' He wasn't interested in who I was, but my name on the timesheet was all that mattered to him.

'Can I walk the new holes?'

Ron Kirby, the designer of Castlemartyr, Skellig Bay and Old Head among others, had been drafted in to design four new holes at the southern end of the course to give more space to the tight and dangerous Corballis.

'Whatever,' came the reply. I took this as a yes.

I carried a 7 iron with me, as golf etiquette dictates, and pocketed a couple of balls so I could try a couple of bump-and-run shots to get a feel for the course. There was a gang of kids ahead of me, playing as a six-ball, so I was surprised when I walked up to the new holes only to be stopped by the course superintendent, standing beside his van.

'Where do you think you're going?' he demanded. Dressed in dark green overalls, this was a man who had spent his working life outdoors and had the weather-beaten face to prove it.

I hadn't expected anything quite so abrupt.

'I'm going to walk the new holes.'

'Are you now?' Hands on hips. 'And who said you could do that?'

'The lad in the shop. He said it would be OK. I'm just walking them,' I reiterated.

'He doesn't have the authority to give you permission. I'll have words with him later.' He glared at me and then looked at the club in my hand. 'Have you paid your green fee?'

'I'm not playing, I'm walking the course for a book I'm writing.'

He wasn't remotely interested. 'For someone walking the course, you're playing a lot of shots.'

I was getting angry.

'I played two shots into that green,' I retorted, indicating the 3rd hole behind me. 'I haven't hit another shot. Now, am I allowed to walk the new holes or not?'

He drew himself up to his full height, which still worked out at an inch shorter than me – and I'm short – and delivered a classic.

'I've been a superintendent here for thirty years, and I have never been spoken to like that before.'

He was only doing his job, but I dearly wanted to tell him

where to stick his thirty years. Instead I tried a different approach. 'I'm reviewing golf courses and it would really help if I could see the new holes. I didn't mean to upset anyone.'

'Fine,' he humphed, 'but keep off the fairways and greens. They're still bedding in.'

He carried on with the glaring and then climbed into his van. He reversed down the hill and drove straight across the 3rd fairway and past the six-ball of kids playing the 8th.

Next door, The Island Golf Club is Dublin's most exciting links course yet it keeps its light well and truly hidden. The course grabs you by the throat, holds on tight and then sucker-punches you with the Index 1 18th. I played the course on a bright, brisk day, with two Americans. Jack and Jon were in Ireland for the first time, playing eight rounds in eight days, finishing at The Island.

Both men wore t-shirts and sleeveless jumpers in the early morning sunshine. Jon was the shape of a rugby prop and he sported a grey goatee. He was middle-aged and the younger of the two by maybe fifteen years. Jack was taller, thinner and his goatee was white, as was the hair squeezing out from under his cap. Jack had turned out in shorts.

'That,' I said, pointing to tanned Phoenix legs, 'is ambitious.'

Considering the temperatures that Phoenix, Arizona, experiences, I was surprised Jack wasn't wearing a fur coat and an electric blanket.

My brother-in-law Perry went to Phoenix on business a few years back. He was trying to find his way to the hotel and stood on a street corner figuring out which way to turn. It was the middle of the day and over 40 °C. A man walked past.

'You must be a tourist,' the man said.

'How can you tell?' asked Perry.

'You're standing still. Stay there any longer and your shoes will melt.'

Back in the bar after our round, I asked Jack and Jon for the highlights of their trip.

'The Guinness,' joked Jon, becoming an honorary Irishman in the blink of an eye.

5

Monkeys, Snails and Other Duds

'Columbus went around the world in 1492. That isn't a lot
of strokes when you consider the course.'

LEE TREVINO

The day job had taken over and two weeks at home were
required to clear my desk. It was good to spend time with those
who mattered most and I enjoyed being free of the fairways. I
worked during the day and spent the evenings planning a big
trip west. I was revisiting County Cork, before driving into
Kerry, and then up through Clare and Galway. It was peak
golfing season. Fairways would be busy and clubhouses open
late. I would be taking in many of the greatest links courses on
earth, and several parklands of particular Irish acclaim. One of
these parklands was where I started.

'What time are you playing tomorrow?' Seamus asked,
leaning across the table in one of the most luxurious
clubhouse lounges I have ever encountered.

I had driven west from Wexford, through Waterford and
on to Fota Island, just east of Cork city.

'Seven fifteen,' I replied, thinking that I was being offered his company for the morning round. Playing off two, Seamus, Fota Island's Director of Golf, would know the place intimately. Sadly, I was wrong.

'That's a shame. You'll be too early to hear the monkeys being fed.'

'Excuse me?'

'The monkeys in Fota Wildlife Park. It's behind the 4th green and they get fed at ten in the morning. Make one hell of a racket. We've had visitors come running back to the clubhouse swearing that people are being murdered on the other side of the trees.' Seamus paused and smiled. 'And then there are the lemurs.'

He was baiting me.

'They escape from time to time and like to gather around the 4th green. It's not a hazard you encounter every day.'

The Wildlife Park was silent as I walked by . . . not even a brace of balls fired over the trees got a response. No doubt the monkeys turned up by the green in the afternoon to sell them back to some hapless golfer.

Finding Mahon Municipal Golf Club that evening was more luck than skill. It's not far from Fota Island and Cork Golf Club, but it wasn't signposted from the South Ring Road. The laneway to the club doesn't help either, being so narrow that there's always a thought in the back of your mind that you might have to reverse the same way. But the golf course appeared soon enough, then the Blackrock Inn and finally the clubhouse. Rather conveniently, the distance between the latter two is 20 yards.

I had been instructed to get a key from Peter to let myself onto the course in the morning. It is, I am happy to say, the only club in Ireland that locks its course up at night.

Then it was off to the pub. I was chuckling away at how I had come from the best course in the region to a humble municipal at the other end of the scale where the place got locked up every night. Perhaps I looked like I was barking mad, sitting alone with a laptop, laughing to myself, because two lads came across and asked me what I was doing. Neither of them was a golfer, so my quest was lost on them.

'Golf? Sure, that's not a real sport, boy,' said one.

'If you want to do something with a stick, you need to be hurling. That's a real game, for real men,' continued the other.

They were Cork GAA men. Not a problem, Wexford has a GAA team too, although over the course of a few pints the lads were keen to convince me otherwise. To give the lads their due, Cork have won the All-Ireland senior championship ten times in the last forty years; Wexford won it once.

On my travels, I worked on the simple hypothesis that when I played twice a day, I would have the course to myself in the morning and I'd hook up with someone in the afternoon. A sensible assumption when you tee off at around 7 a.m., but Mahon had a surprise in store. At 6.30 a.m., a car pulled up next to the camper van and I heard the unmistakable sound of clubs being unloaded. I looked under the blinds and saw a man hunched forward as he tied his shoes. I was tempted to ask if he fancied a round but, as it turned out, I would never have managed to keep up. This was my first glimpse of the Running Man of Mahon.

By 7 a.m. I was on the 1st tee, somewhat confused. It was a sunny morning, with heavy dew on the ground. The dew clearly showed the tracks of the mystery man – only there appeared to be more than one. Two or three sets of footprints headed off in different directions. I looked back at the car park, but ours were the only two vehicles.

Mahon may be a short, humble municipal course but it is cracking fun. I was so wrapped up in the course that I had forgotten about the early morning golfer by the 6th hole. I walked onto the tee and was admiring the shot to come when a man appeared behind the green. He was heading up the 7th.

I was speechless. The man was running. He had a club in his hand and I looked back to the 7th tee where his golf bag remained. I vaguely raised my arm to point out the obvious, but thought better of it. So I watched in amazement as the man ran to his ball, looked at it, turned and then ran back for his trolley. He continued running, pulling the trolley to the ball, hitting his second shot and then repeating the process, running up and then back.

'Beautiful day,' he called out as he went behind the 6th green for the third time. I managed a 'you-must-be-insane' type of wave before he disappeared. I saw him again a couple of times, always in the distance, always running.

'Oh, that's John Horgan,' Peter in the shop told me later. 'He's sixty-seven and plays here two or three times a week. It's just the way he likes to play golf.'

I could see why he played alone.

At nearby Douglas Golf Club I joined some English lads who were on a mad dash of golf, playing five rounds in three days. They were reluctant to stay in the clubhouse bar afterwards, complaining the place was too stuffy. Douglas is old school (established in 1909), with dark carpets infested with swirling shapes, heavy doors that creak, and a visitors' bar and a members' bar well separated by long-held protocol. I pulled out my laptop and was looking for a plug when I realised that this was the kind of place where using such modern technology might be frowned upon. I queried it with the bar lady. She looked around carefully and then shook her head. 'Best not,' she said with an apologetic smile.

The thing is, I have no problem with this. If a club has a rule that you don't use laptops, mobile phones or other electronic devices then that's their policy. In the same way, you should accept a club's policy when they ask you not to wear jeans on the course or baseball caps in the bar. It's their clubhouse and their course. If you want to play there then abide by their rules. I grant you, some of the rules are enforced with unnecessary harshness, like the time some friends arrived late at Royal County Down and, in order to make their tee time, they changed their shoes in the car park. Out marched an RCD employee to tell them this was forbidden and that they were no longer welcome to play. A bit severe for changing shoes but RCD has had many gripes aimed at it over the years. My favourite involved Gary Player. The story goes that Player arrived to play in County Down as a five-time Major winner, only to be approached by an elderly member. Thinking he was going to be congratulated or asked for an autograph, Player was stumped when the old member made it clear that Player wasn't welcome. Why? Because Player had taken the elderly gent's preferred tee time.

Such scenarios are not exclusive to the posh clubs. Far from it as I was about to discover.

'You almost *^$@^*% killed me,' the man roared. 'Why didn't you *^%!*^ shout "fore"?'

When you play a few hundred golf courses in a short amount of time you expect to have run-ins with fellow golfers. I was lucky to have only two or three, and Monkstown Golf Club was the most confrontational.

The deal I struck with most golf clubs was a simple one: I'd turn up the night before in Rusty and then play early in the morning before any other golfers arrived, but after the greenkeepers had done their work. For the most part it worked very well. At Monkstown, however, unbeknownst to me someone had started at the 10th. Not knowing the course and not knowing anyone was ahead of me, a wayward drive into the trees on the 11th didn't cause me any concern . . . not until I reached my ball and a very angry member who was standing over it. He was a solid, middle-aged man with greying hair and a poor fashion sense, much like my own. His face was flushed while his eyeballs threatened to pop out and join my ball. He was playing the 15th which runs parallel to the hole I was playing and he was livid.

The abuse I received was disproportionate to the crime because my ball was in the trees and nowhere near his fairway, but the way he was holding his 7 iron inspired me to apologise quickly and move on. He was four holes ahead of me, so I didn't expect to meet him again.

Unfortunately, he'd parked next to the camper van and he was changing his shoes when I finished my round. The 'conversation' started again, with renewed vigour as he realised I wasn't a member. Like most golfers I have been caught out by not calling 'Fore' when I should have, or almost been hit by someone failing to shout a warning, but it had never resulted in this type of confrontation. I concluded that he had suffered the fright of his life – either that or he was the obnoxious golfer who is required by law in every club.

'Kevin,' a voice called from behind.

I turned to see Derry, an elderly golfer who had caught up with me on the 18th (after someone else had cut in), waving me inside. I went willingly.

Derry is a knowledgeable man. He spoke at length about the demise of Cork's Harbour Point Golf Club and how the members had lost out to an ambitious landowner. As was common at the time, if you owned green space in a suitable location you could make your fortune by building and selling houses. Harbour Point, it appeared, was going to suffer that fate. Unlike Bray and Dun Laoghaire Golf Clubs, which sold their courses on the condition a new course was built for them, Harbour Point members were left high and dry. On hearing that I was on my way to play Ballybunion and Lahinch, Derry was keen to discuss Ivan Morris's book *Only Golf Spoken Here*, in which Morris compares the courses at the end of the book, and rates Lahinch higher. Derry didn't agree, but he urged me to get my hands on the book as it was a 'damn fine read'.

I had the book sitting in the cupboard of the camper van, and the pages were well thumbed over the coming days.

Derry wished me luck on the rest of my trip and recommended that I play from the back tees on the 18th at Old Head of Kinsale . . . 'if you've got the balls'.

Cork, like Donegal and Kerry, is one of Ireland's most stunning counties. The landscape, the villages, the food – they're all good and the farther west you go, the better they get.

Kinsale is one of the best-known destinations. It is a pretty fishing village about 30 kilometres southwest of Monkstown Golf Club. The streets are crammed with colourful houses, artists' studios, a bustling harbour and enough restaurants to see you eating some place different every night for a month. Walking around the village it is easy to see what draws people here. During tourism season the population doubles or even trebles. There's a buzz to the place that comes not just from the people but from the village itself. I strolled along Main Street, admiring the window displays of art, photography and pottery, until I finally gave in to my stomach's rumbling.

Just off the Main Street, next to a small park, I was drawn to the lunchtime smells drifting out of the Fishy Fishy restaurant. I've never been a big fan of fish, but this was a fishing village . . . if I couldn't get good fish here, what hope was there!

Seafood chowder was followed by the subtly-named Fishy Fishy Pie. The awards on the wall made it clear that this was a highly regarded restaurant and I concurred wholeheartedly. I'd never tasted anything like the food, and it was so relaxed that three hours passed in no time. A lazy day never hurt anyone. I had nowhere to be and I was wrapped up nicely in a corner with a book. As I paid the bill I looked at my watch and wondered if it would be rude to ask if I could stay until they started serving dinner.

I left the village early the next day, driving towards the Old Head of Kinsale and one of the world's great golf experiences. It started with a perfect sunrise, a ball of orange rising from the ocean to create an idyllic, golden landscape that led me on to the golf resort.

Old Head is probably Ireland's most exclusive and dramatic resort, flowing over a headland that juts out into the Atlantic. From the restaurant looking out over the 18th to the ocean, to the changing rooms, to the Starter greeting you with a clutch of tees and markers in hand, you know these are moments to be cherished. I was certainly cherishing mine until the Starter stuck his hand through a hole in a rock, while looking at me expectantly.

'It's the Rock of Accord,' he said by way of explanation. Oh boy!

I shook hands and then reciprocated. No doubt the Americans love this flourish but me, not so much. I came to play golf, not go fisting my way through a lump of stone.

Old Head doesn't allow trolleys on its velvet fairways so

I splashed out and got myself a caddie. He stood beside me as I performed this odd ritual, not saying a word.

But that didn't last long. Patrick was a talker. Once he'd established that I knew which end of the club to hold, he was away. Tall, skinny, in his twenties, with a foppish mop of black hair that would have made Starsky nervous, Patrick hailed from Pittsburgh.

'Yeah,' he said as if we were in the middle of a conversation. 'I came to Ireland on holiday last year. I fell in love and decided to stay.'

We were only approaching the 2nd tee, and we were discussing his love life already. That didn't bode well. Fortunately, the view from the 2nd tee box is a conversation stopper. You come out of tall pampas grasses and you're on a tee that sits above the cliffs. The roar of the ocean rises up to you and the fairway curves around the edge of the sheer drop to a green that looks as if it might topple into the sea at any moment. It is breathtaking and my jaw hitting the ground brought Patrick back to earth.

He pointed out to sea, between the peninsula and the headlands that lay to the east. 'The *Lusitania* sank over there, about 10 miles out, after it was torpedoed by a German submarine in 1915. Almost 1,200 people were lost.'

The loss of over a hundred Americans on board was the catalyst that drew America into the First World War. It's hard to believe that such a tragedy and such consequences could come from this peaceful, isolated place.

Patrick was reeling it off with a style and rhythm that suggested he had the story down pat and had been regurgitating it daily. At Old Head, caddies double as tour guides. Many of the visitors who play here are American, so local history always adds colour to the round and, perhaps, a different colour to the money they get tipped.

'How good are the guys you caddie for?' I asked.

He looked around carefully, judging how far the wind could carry his next words.

'Pretty crap. You're the first decent golfer I've caddied for in weeks.' He elaborated, providing details of double-bagging (which is carrying two bags and not some unusual sexual practice), spending hours in the rough searching for balls that everyone knew had gone over the cliff, and trying to convince over-optimistic golfers that a 9 iron won't get them to the green 200 yards away, even with a force 10 gale at their back.

'I had this couple a few days ago,' he continued. 'Lovely people, but not golfers. She had never played in her life but she turned up with all the gear. Pink bag, pink clothes, pink shoes, pink grips. Even her balls were pink! And that's not something you'll hear me say again in this lifetime or the next.' He shook his head sadly. 'Such a waste, but her husband took me to one side and told me to look after her – which I guess was his way of saying he wanted to focus on his own game.'

I saw his rationale.

'So I looked after her all day, was really positive and enthusiastic, gave her tips all the way round. It was a laugh, believe me, and she had a fab time. And it was worth it. At the end her husband was delighted and gave me the biggest tip I've ever had.'

I couldn't resist. 'How much?'

He wouldn't tell me, other than to use the word 'huge'. Shortly thereafter we were back to his love life.

The object of Patrick's affection had not returned his amorous advances or, to be less subtle, she'd dumped him once he started getting serious. The girl had seen it as a holiday romance; Patrick had seen it as a lifelong partnership. He was an intense young man, for sure, and by trying to convince me of his own self-worth it was evident that his intensity had been the cause of his self-destruction.

'But I won't give up. I'll win her back.' Each of his words was cut with angst.

The boy needed a good slap and a 'wake up and smell the coffee' speech, but mention of the coffee might induce a reverie about making her breakfast after a night of passion. No, I kept my mouth shut as we stood on the 11th green.

'I did everything for her. I cycled miles to her house, made friends with her family – do you need a line on that putt? – called her every day, left presents – hit it with pace just outside the left edge – but she stopped returning my calls.'

Is anyone else shocked by this?

We had reached the 12th tee on the edge of the cliffs and I could see nowhere to aim my drive. Some people gripe about the design of Old Head, claiming that the owners missed the opportunity to create something epic. Hogwash. If the 12th isn't epic, I don't know what is. Called Razor's Edge, it is a par five that doglegs around the cliffs, demanding that you drive over the yawning chasm to reach a fairway you can't see above you. Patrick guided me expertly, my drive finding the centre of the fairway.

I was left with 200 yards straight to the green, the cliffs all along the left. A 9 iron perhaps?

'What are you thinking?' Patrick asked, rifling through my bag.

'Will I reach the green with anything in there?'

'No. With that wind off the sea it's playing 250 yards.'

'A 3 iron then.'

He handed me the club, a slight smirk indicating he had been through this before.

I sighed. 'OK, what?' I asked as I took my stance.

115

He shrugged, enjoying himself. You need to aim left a bit . . . a bit more . . . a bit more.'

I obeyed until he had me pointing out to sea, almost at 90 degrees to the green. 'Are you serious?' I asked incredulously.

'Trust me.'

And I did, hitting indisputably the best shot of my life. The ball sailed low and fast out to sea, over the cliff's edge and the angry ocean, and above the hordes of screeching gulls. The wind toyed with it, lifting it upwards and then slapping it back towards the land. Against the black cliffs it was a beautiful thing to watch as it honed in on the fairway, touching down short of the green.

'Wow' was all I could manage, but Patrick was already walking towards the green, well used to seeing the seeds of his advice bear fruit and proving how a caddie can lift your game to a different level.

I did play off the back tees on the 18th, as per Derry's recommendation, and I understood his challenge: the lighthouse rises vertically behind you, the cliffs drop vertically in front of you . . . even reaching the tee box along a narrow path is a lesson in 'whatever-you-do-don't-look-down'. It is not the sort of place to discover you have vertigo.

My morning round at Bandon Golf Club was with Donal Hannon who had been a member for just a year. I felt sorry for him: he was in his late thirties, new to the game and he'd turned up on a Saturday morning hoping to meet some members that he could play with regularly. Instead he gets stuck with a tourist. Still, after a few holes he found his tour guide spiel, although it wasn't quite as polished as Patrick's. As we walked to the 5th, through a wood of oak trees, he mentioned that the local Earl of Bandon had been kidnapped in the 1920s.

'It was 1924, wasn't it?' I asked.

That stumped him. He looked at me with surprise and said he didn't know. But I'd cheated. I'd looked at the Presidents' board in the clubhouse that morning and had seen that between 1909 and 1924, the President was the 4th Earl of Bandon; between 1925 and 1932 it was the 5th Earl.

Unfortunately, my assumption was wrong. The Earl was kidnapped in 1921. It was during the time of the notorious Black and Tans, and an IRA party arrived at Castle Bernard with the intention of kidnapping the 4th Earl, nicknamed 'Buckshot Bandon'. When he couldn't be found, they proceeded to set fire to the castle. The Earl had hidden himself away in the cellar with his family and staff. Once they realised the place was on fire, they promptly revealed themselves in the vain hope that the fire could be extinguished. But it was too late. Oddly, the IRA had removed the furniture in advance of setting the fire . . . whether to steal it or to sit around and watch the castle burn while toasting marshmallows I do not know. And after watching the castle burn to the ground, they still kidnapped the Earl. He was held for three weeks as a bargaining chip to stop the British executing IRA prisoners. The Earl, aged seventy-one, never recovered from the ordeal and died three years later. His heir, the 5th Earl, chose not to rebuild the castle. Instead he built a house within the castle boundary and lived there with his wife until he died in 1979. With no heir, the title died with him.

The reason Donal asked the question became apparent as we arrived on the 5th tee. There, to the right, sit the rather magnificent ruins of Castle Bernard, just out of reach. Through the gaping, glassless windows it is easy to see the trees growing in what must have been elegant rooms. And with the theft of the marble door frame the castle has been left completely naked.

As we walked past at it, Donal wondered why the club wasn't called Castle Bernard Golf Club. Surely that sounded more impressive. And couldn't the castle be turned into a magnificent clubhouse? I agreed with him and thought of the Monkstown Castle restorations. True, at Monkstown the restorations were not for the golf club, but here was a rich piece of Irish history that could be rebuilt . . . although things are rarely that easy.

Donal rushed off after the round to see his son play football, and I headed west on the N71, where I found Amen Corner – Skibbereen-style.

In total, I played half a dozen courses that bragged about their 'Amen Corner'. It started to get as clichéd as 'hidden gem' and 'you'll need every club in your bag' and I learned to take the claim with a large pinch of salt.

In the car park of Skibbereen Golf Club, Arthur walked over and introduced himself. He was a friendly old soul, tall and willowy with grey hair that seemed to attract the breeze. Like so many before and after him, he was amused to see a camper van in his golf club's car park.

'That's a mighty fine way to be getting around the country,' he said, squinting through thick glasses. 'Are ye travelling far?'

We chatted about my travels and that's when he dropped in one of the most famous run of holes in golf:

'We have our own Amen Corner here.' His nod was slow and serious. 'Over there,' he said, pointing away to a hillside. 'Too difficult for a man of my age, but nothing for the likes of a young man. You be sure to remember that when you play it tomorrow.' He looked around and peered down the 18th. 'And watch out for those girl-folk.'

And with that he was on his way.

The Amen Corner holes are on the back nine, a couple of minutes' walk away, stretching up and around a wild hillside, but it is the 2nd hole that captures the imagination. You won't believe it when you stand on the tee but this is a par three, despite no green or flag being visible. In the dull glimmer of sunrise I thought I was going mad and didn't hit a tee shot. I simply walked towards the 3rd tee until I fell into a hollow and the 2nd green broke my fall.

The 'girl-folk' Arthur had referred to were the ladies from Monkstown and Ceann Sibéal golf clubs who were playing three interclub matches. Monkstown achieved a clean sweep and I joined them in the rustic, wooden clubhouse afterwards where they told me about their matches.

'I know who you are,' said one. 'You're that mad one driving around Ireland in a camper van. Playing every course. I read about you in the paper.'

It was the first (and only) time on my travels that somebody knew who I was. And it made a change from being mistaken for Tom Coyne.

Their opponents were getting ready to leave and as Ceann Sibéal was still to come on this trip I thought I'd try and rustle up a playing partner. From what I'd heard I was going to need one.

'Sorry to hear you lost today,' I said as I approached three ladies. 'I'm due in Ceann Sibéal next week, and was wondering if any of you would be interested in playing a round with me.'

Yes, in hindsight, I could have phrased the question less suggestively, but golf promises more inappropriate puns than all other sports combined. It took me a second to figure out why I was getting the silent, hostile stare treatment. I paused, engaged my brain and rephrased the question. Finally, one of them pointed over my shoulder and suggested I talk to their driver, before they walked off. Joe was far more accommodating and a lot less concerned about my turn of phrase. He took my details and said he'd be in touch.

I drove west to Bantry, another of Cork's pretty fishing towns, where the square down by the harbour bursts into life on market day. There's a constant buzz along its streets, too, making it a popular tourist base from which to explore some of Ireland's most beautiful spots. The Sheep's Head peninsula is a beautiful walk to the southwest of the town, stretching out to a lighthouse where red railings contrast sharply against the Atlantic Ocean. The next finger of land to the south is the Mizen Head peninsula, where I spent my summers as a young boy, bashing a ball around the 9-hole Barley Cove course. With its infestation of cowpat hazards, lift, clean and drop was required on most holes. If you ended up on an old, crusty cowpat you could elect to play it . . . if you were that stupid. I tried once, on one of my first visits, and learned a valuable lesson: if you're trying to be clever, don't do it on the 1st hole, because you have to live with the consequences for the rest of the round. My dad was still laughing that night at dinner and I never wore those trousers again.

Farther along this jigsaw-edged coastline is a rather special place by the name of Garinish Island. Often called Ilnacullin, 'island of holly', it covers 37 acres and sits regally in Glengarriff Harbour. Much of it is home to a beautiful garden, started some eighty years ago and now entrusted to the care of the Office of Public Works. Thanks to its sheltered location, the island benefits from the warm Gulf Stream, creating a perfect environment for ornamental plants from around the world. Come in May and enjoy the rhododendrons and azaleas in full flower. It's an explosion of colour and fragrances that dazzles the senses.

I had to pay twice to get in (once for the small ferry, once for the gardens) but it was well worth it. The ferry was a sweet trip and took ten minutes, including a quick circuit of rocks layered in seals. They were so utterly bored by the day's events, they refused to acknowledge us. A woman, French I think, was determined to get herself in the frame as her husband snapped off photos. They were barging people out of the way to get the best view of the seals, utterly oblivious to the ruckus they were causing. At one point she leaned precariously over the gunwale and I took advantage, walking over and planting my foot on her plump rump. I booted her out of the boat. The splash attracted the seals who slid off the rocks and headed our way. We all applauded as the seals enjoyed a tasty mid-morning snack. The husband even took photographs to remember the occasion.

An active imagination is a wonderful thing and, judging by the furious expressions directed at the couple, the other passengers were on the same wavelength as me.

After an uneventful ferry trip back to the mainland I set off for Kenmare. I was taking the road less travelled, following the R572 that hovers above glorious views of Bantry Bay, all the way to Castletownbere. At least, that was my plan. As I approached Adrigole, a sign for Healy Pass flashed by. Why not? I thought, and hung a right.

The dictionary defines hindsight thus: the sight of your behind as you make a complete ass of yourself. It was an apt description of my decision-making that day.

From Adrigole I drove along a small lane, trees towering above. There was a school to my left and two children ran over waving their arms and shouting. I waved back. The trees ended, almost in fright, and the smile slipped from my face as the mountains appeared above me. This is a desolate place where fields are filled with vast stones, scattered as if from a giant's hand. Hillsides of rock rose left and right, leaving barely enough room for the narrow road that winds its way ever upwards. I should never have started the ascent and by the time I was halfway up, I was reduced to second gear. It was agonisingly slow and two thoughts occurred to me: what if someone started coming the other way; and what if I had to reverse. I was genuinely terrified. The sharp bends only compounded the problem and there were times when I thought I'd have to get out and push to save the camper going backwards. I realised now that the kids weren't waving at me – they were warning me.

I persevered. It was hard to believe that the distance from Adrigole in County Cork to Lauragh Bridge in County Kerry is just 8 miles because fifteen minutes later, I hadn't even gone a mile. The rev counter was tipping the red and the temperature gauge was rising. Not that I could see them for the fear of taking my eyes off the road . . . that and the sweat pouring down my face. Ahead, I caught sight of another vehicle approaching the top, going as slowly as me. It gave me hope. I kept my foot down and the prayer count up.

When I reached the utopia of level ground, I pulled over and stumbled out. I looked back down the valley into Cork, catching my breath, then turned and headed to the other side. I was greeted by views of water, mountains and forests. This was County Kerry; this was The Kingdom.

My troublesome but scenic route over the Healy Pass in the Caha Mountains rises to 1,100 feet, and marks the boundary between counties Cork and Kerry. It was built during the Famine, in 1847, and owes its existence to Timothy Michael Healy, who was born in Cork and became the first Governor General of Ireland. He died in March 1931, and the road was named after him four weeks later. If you come this way, be sure to look for the Flat Rock at the top of the pass. Funeral processions between the two counties would meet and stop here, using the stone to pass the coffin from one side of the border to the other.

I know this because I looked it up on the Internet as Rusty and I sat at the top of the mountain, both of us recovering from the ordeal.

Cork has its pretty villages and towns, and Kerry's Kenmare is well able to match them. It's a bustling little place, its buildings of different colours adding splashes of interest to the three main streets, while small local businesses have an approach to shop-window displays that would give Brown Thomas a heart attack. Tourists from across the world throng the streets and wander about as if they're on a movie set, performing double-takes and dramatic pauses. It all gives Kenmare a vibrancy that's hard to resist.

On the outskirts of town, resting on the edge of the Roughty River, is Kenmare Golf Club. It boasts an authentic Indian hunting lodge as its clubhouse. White wooden boards on the outside, a veranda running across the front and a wooden interior all made for a very colonial atmosphere. The gang of English lads on the veranda were right at home.

When Lord Lansdowne brought the lodge back to Ireland in the early 1900s, and later gifted it to the golf club, I'm sure he didn't expect one of the chief residents to be a robin. The happy little bird was hopping about under the tables foraging for food, with not a care in the world. It wasn't remotely bothered when the English golfers started throwing crumbs at it. One of the lads walked past me on his way to the bar and the bird hopped past my feet and followed him. It flew up onto the Heineken tap, just a couple of feet from where he was standing.

'I'll have a pint,' he said to the robin. The robin flew off into the back.

The guy looked at me with a dead straight face: 'Birds behind the bar these days.'

I joined them for a drink, which turned into a few, and I heard about their Irish golfing exploits as well as a heated debate on the merits of Guinness versus Murphy's Stout.

'There is nothing as pure or as perfect as a pint of Guinness poured in Ireland,' said Danny, although not as coherently as that.

'I'm for Murphy's,' countered Simon. 'I wouldn't pour a pint of Guinness on you if you were on fire.'

Danny was less than impressed.

I intervened. 'You're talking about Irish Guinness, aren't you, Danny? Not that English dishwater stuff.'

He pointed at me, nodded once. 'That's what I said.' He turned to Simon. 'There you go. Buy that man a drink.'

If pints were consumed purely by how timeless and how desirable they look, men in Ireland would be drunk on the stuff every night. The velvet black body and rich creamy mane is irresistible. Wherever I went, I watched men, young and old, hovering at the bar as the Guinness settled in the glass, a look of pure love on their faces. Is it any wonder it's one of Ireland's most formidable exports and has been for 200 years. Sales of Guinness may have declined in recent years, but they are still worth around €2 billion annually.

In the centre of the table a pint glass was half-full of coins and notes.

I nodded towards it. 'What gives?'

Simon leaned his considerable bulk forward, the chair creaking in complaint. He was probably the most sober one of the group. Probably. 'That's our swear box. We started off with this great plan that every time someone got a birdie, everyone else had to put a euro in the pot. An eagle was two euro. The idea was to get enough cash for a big blow out on our last night.'

I should have put them in touch with the boys from Mount Wolseley. One eagle would have had them tripping the light fantastic.

'Only problem was,' Simon continued, 'it hasn't worked out too well cos we've been playing utter shite.'

There was a roar of disapproval from the others and they started chanting: 'In the box, in the box', until Simon took a Euro and added it to the pint glass.

Simon was in his late twenties, like the rest of his companions, with most of his hair shaved off. 'So yours truly came up with this idea of a swear box. A Euro per word. There's probably a hundred quid in there and most of it's mine.'

We drank for a while and by the time the clubhouse closed and we were all hoiked out into the car park I'd added a few Euro to the pint glass myself. I wasn't happy. Once they realised that talking politics brought out the worst in me, they never let up.

Read any travel book about Ireland and there will be direct or veiled references to our drinking culture. We enjoy a drink, it's true. Some of us are sensible about it, but plenty are not. In one clubhouse they had a radio switched on to RTÉ Radio 1's morning show. A mother of five boys was complaining that her sons could no longer go to the pub, enjoy a perfectly acceptable eight pints and then drive home as they were entitled to do. 'Where's the harm in that?' she moaned. 'Sure, it's an absolute disgrace, this random breathalysing thing stopping my boys from having a good time.'

I did plenty of drinking on my travels but it's not exactly a cheap business. My most costly experience came at one of those country courses that overflows with a friendly, family atmosphere and where the pace of life is slow enough to confuse your watch. Time doesn't quite stand still but you'll find it sitting comfortably by the bar and with no inclination to rush.

After my round I walked in to an empty clubhouse. Small and cosy, the carpet was of a pattern and colour that suggested someone had spilled brown paint before setting Michael Flatley loose on the floor. I wasn't going to be fussy about what I drank as I strolled over to the elderly lady behind the bar. The wrinkles on her face suggested that smiling was what she did best and she beamed at me. How was my game, she wanted to know. Had I come far? What did I think of the club?

'Now then love, what can I get you?' she asked after our golf chatter had run its course.

'A Heineken shandy would be lovely.' I tried not to smack my lips.

'Right.' She turned away but then she did the oddest thing. She stood completely still for a few seconds, caught in her own personal time warp, before she grabbed a glass and started pouring me a pint of Budweiser. No bother, I thought, a shandy's a shandy. But she didn't stop, and placed a full pint on the counter.

She paused again. She looked at me, I looked at her. Our eyes met.

'Oh no,' she said, a hint of despair in her voice. 'That's wrong.'

I was parched. I needed a drink. I would have drunk dishwater at that point so I watched in open-mouthed horror as she poured the pint down the sink.

'Heineken,' she said to herself. 'Heineken.' She paused, reached for a fresh glass and poured the Heineken. All the way to the top.

She looked at me. I looked at her.

'What was it you wanted?' she asked.

'A shandy, but that's . . .'

Too late. The pint went the way of the first one.

She hesitated, the freeze button pressed once again. 'Right,' she said when she snapped out of it. 'Shandy,' she reminded herself, looking around. 'Lemonade.'

There were two lemonade bottles standing between us but she turned and disappeared for a few moments, returning with a full one. She cracked it open and started pouring it into a third glass. All the way to the top.

She paused. Our eyes meet. She shook her head once and poured it down the drain without a word. I decided that this was no time to interfere as she grabbed a new glass, poured the Heineken about three quarters of the way up the glass and placed it carefully on the counter. In went the lemonade.

'Perfect. Thank you,' I said as she pushed the glass towards me. In return I handed her a €20 note.

She turned to the till, opened it, tucked the €20 away and then closed it. Another long pause. Then she turned around.

She looked at me, I looked at her. Our eyes met and she smiled.

'Now then love,' she said, 'what can I get you?'

The following morning at Kenmare, I played with Steve, Peter and Tom – an Irishman, an Englishman and, sadly, a Canadian. I would have preferred a Scotsman to complete the triumvirate but, as it turned out, Tom was the joker of the group. Aged well over seventy, they played the full eighteen comfortably, drifting from the old, pretty nine, to the hilly new nine.

Peter was rake thin and despite a slight stoop he was still over six feet tall. His golf was slow, his swing a touch frail and his voice the sound of two tons of gravel. There aren't many sports that you can still play in your eighties, still enjoy yourself and give your friends all kinds of grief. It was one of the slowest and most enjoyable rounds I played. These guys got together every week during the summer when Tom was over from the States.

'The States?' I queried. 'I thought you said you were from Canada.'

Tom looked sheepish but confessed to being American. With the White House screwing up the world he preferred not to tell people his true nationality. I couldn't blame him.

When you consider the love affair that exists between Ireland and the USA, it is remarkable how one man . . . and by one man I mean George W. Bush . . . soured worldwide relations to such an extent.

The infamous Ring of Kerry, the N70, is not to be trifled with at the best of times, but in the dark you might as well try steering with your teeth for all the control you'll have. I was heading for Waterville, 60 kilometres west, and dusk was looming. It doesn't sound far, but on these roads the camper van was likely to take flight at any speed over 50 km/h. Enthusiastic tourists would do well to remember that. Quite frankly, if you are going to hire a car for this trip you might as well take a brick to the undercarriage before you leave the airport car park. Try to go too fast and it will rattleyou from your teeth to your testicles. I have a suggestion for Kerry County Council: repair the road properly and give the tourists a journey to remember, rather than a road to forget.

Roads aside, the Ring of Kerry is a beautiful drive of 179

kilometres. It skirts the Iveragh Peninsula, and its glorious views on land and out to sea attract tourists from near and far. The MacGillycuddy's Reeks are majestic mountains to the northeast of the ring (and form evocative backdrops for Killarney and Beaufort Golf Clubs), and mountains run almost all the way to the peninsula's western tip. There are dozens of lakes that sparkle like silver while, out to sea, the razor-like Skellig Rocks pierce the skyline.

It gets so busy that tour buses are allowed to drive in only one direction (anti-clockwise) to ensure a smooth flow of traffic and to avoid the endless stand-offs that would ensue. With only a vertical wall of rock or a sheer drop as the options in some places, it is not a stand-off you want to encounter.

It was dark when I reached Waterville. My parking spot for the night was the Waterville Lake Hotel, an eighty-room hotel that dates back to the 1970s. It was late May, but the place looked abandoned. There was not a single vehicle in the car park and, apart from the security light that snapped on and blinded me as I approached the doors, the hotel was wrapped in darkness. It felt like a scene from *The Shining*.

I walked into a dim foyer. 'Hello.'

'Hello!' came back. The volume took me by surprise as a young woman shot through from a room behind the desk, all smiles and waves. 'How are you today? Did you find us all right? I know the roads aren't the best, but at least it's quiet this time of year. You're early, Mr O'Neill. Did you have a good journey down from the airport?'

One breathless welcome, Irish style.

'I'm not Mr O'Neill,' I replied.

'Oh,' she said, the question mark in her voice followed by an inquisitive head tilt. 'We're only expecting one tonight.'

I introduced myself and explained that I was staying in the car park in my camper van.

Nope, that didn't register with Vivienne, but she seemed happy enough to let me stay. Mr O'Neill, it transpired, was a Canadian – allegedly – who was flying in for a wedding in two days' time. A party for a hundred people was due that night.

The woman was nuts. It was 7.30 p.m., not a soul stirred and here she was predicting a big shindig. Not to mention that the restaurant was closed.

'The chef's not in until nine. You could try the village.' Vivienne suggested the Lobster Bar and then returned into the darkness.

Like much of Waterville village, the pub is on one side of the street, with the stunning views of Ballinskelligs Bay right outside the door. Between the houses and the bay is a pretty, green promenade with one permanent visitor. A bronze statue of Charlie Chaplin stands on the path and can often be seen draped in a tourist or two, hugging him, kissing him or striking his famous pose. He used to come to Waterville on holiday and now he's a permanent fixture.

Inside the Lobster Bar it was busy. I found an alcove and settled in to write my reviews, but spent most of the time watching two old men at the bar. They were dressed in jumpers and jackets, in that informal, smart look of the country. One had a head of silver hair that had recently been dragged through a bush backwards; the other was completely bald. And yet, beside their half-drunk pints of plain sat two identical flat caps. The caps didn't move during the evening as glasses came and went, and the way they drank their pints was further proof that there is an unbreakable bond between a man and his pint of Guinness. Love was in the air and in the bottom of the glass, too.

I returned to the hotel about two hours later and the car park was packed, the hotel lit up like a Christmas tree, and a fair old racket of conversation and music spilling from the open windows. I didn't venture in but leaned against the camper van and watched the shadows flicker across the hotel ceiling, smiling at how quickly the Irish can get a party started. If only George W. Bush had asked us to lead the Iraq invasion, things might have been a lot different . . . and Guinness profits would be through the roof.

It began at 3 a.m., so loud and heavy that the camper van vibrated. It was the kind of deluge that thunders down relentlessly and pierces your skull if you're foolish enough to step outside. Around here they call it rain; in most other places it would be called punishment. Put a golfer out in that and he'll be begging for mercy inside five minutes. I stared at the ceiling and decided it couldn't last long.

My 7 a.m. tee time came and went in a squall that turned the car park into a lake.

Not long after, a car appeared and drove slowly towards me, the water parting in waves around it. Jim O'Brien, the golf club's general manager, pulled up beside me, wound down the window less than an inch and introduced himself by shouting through the gap. I shouted back and ventured forth, trying to balance in the camper's doorway and step into the car without letting my feet sink underwater. Jim parked as close to the hotel as possible but we both got soaked as we ran inside. We stood in the lobby trying to shake ourselves off while Vivienne laughed at us.

Somehow, when you play golf in the rain, you're prepared for the unpleasant sensation of water trickling down the back of your neck. You don't know when it will happen, but you know it will. It goes with the territory. Stepping into a hotel feeling like you've just taken a shower in your clothes, with a waterfall spilling down your neck, is a different matter entirely.

We found some soft armchairs and settled in. I only had Skellig Bay Golf Club to play that day, so I wasn't unduly concerned. I still believed the rain had to stop soon.

Jim has been in the golf game in Ireland for a very long time. So long that he can boast memberships at seventeen golf clubs in Munster. It's an impressive list that includes Mallow, Cork, Lahinch and Waterville, which he regards as the best he's ever played.

Skellig Bay was a new course and there were two things that intrigued me: the course's stone walls and the rearing white horse that adorned the club's crest.

'Will I be seeing that horse anywhere during the round?' I enquired.

'Of a fashion.' Jim then explained that the crest's origins were in Irish myth.

The 15th is called *Tír na nÓg*. The village of Waterville provides a postcard backdrop while Ballinskelligs Bay sweeps in to the left. The myth tells of Oisín, the son of Fionn MacCumhaill, leaving Ireland from Rossbeigh Strand for *Tír na nÓg* (Land of Eternal Youth). After 300 years he yearns to return, and he appears riding over the waves of Ballinskelligs Bay on a white horse.

There will always be beautiful courses in Ireland, with flowing fairways weaving through woods, around lakes, over dunes and across cliffs, and where the air is fresh, raw and inspiring. There will always be incredible views of dappled mountains and valleys that come alive in the sunlight, oceans that shimmer and trees that creak and groan in the wind. Standing on a tee box with these elements around you makes you realise how good it is to be alive. But when you find something that is so different to everywhere else, it creates a new category of desirability in your brain's filing system. Skellig Bay is that different. Where else will you be led out onto a beautiful headland with tall stone cairns and endless views over the sea? Where else will you find mile after mile of drystone walls shepherding your every step, leading you through what were once fields of pasture but are now lush, green fairways?

When you travel through Ireland's countryside you will see these beautiful walls, which date back to the Iron Age. How many miles is anyone's guess but, to put it in perspective, Inishmore (the largest of the Aran Islands) is 8 miles long and has 1,400 miles of stone walls. These walls are quintessentially Irish and I found them a reassuring sight: cattle scratching their necks on stone; horses peering over them; and farmers striding alongside, heading from field to field, stick in hand, cap on head, dog at heel.

You see drystone walls climbing mountainsides in perfect straight lines and you ask yourself how they got the stone up there. It must have been back-breaking work, but the walls have stood the test of time. And now, in the twenty-first century, they're being used to define golf holes at Skellig Bay.

I didn't get to see any of Ireland's beauty on that day because it wasn't until 6 p.m., fifteen hours after it started, that the sky finally ran out of rain.

Of the many golf courses on my bucket list, Waterville was near the top. It's on the other side of the village to Skellig Bay, but it enjoys the same striking landscapes.

Almost exactly ten years before, I went to Waterville Golf Club with my best friend Charlie to play a course he had described as heavenly. Our round lasted less than a minute. We walked into the clubhouse and promptly stepped out again after being told the green fee was €65. Neither of us was in a job that justified such expense, and my bride of less than a week was losing patience. Golfing while on honeymoon is a tough sell.

On this occasion, Noel Cronin offered Charlie and me complimentary green fees. Noel held the position of general manager for what seemed like an eternity – certainly back to the time of Fionn MacCumhaill – and during his tenure he was as much a part of the club as the golf course itself. Singling him out and drawing on his wealth of stories became an essential part of playing there.

Charlie arrived shortly after me and he started laughing as he stepped into the camper. Words like 'piece of junk' and 'it smells' were tossed around as he stood with his hands on hips, trying not to touch anything. But then Charlie and I have been competing against each other for over thirty years, and if there's ever an opportunity for a put down, one of us will surely take it. That's the nature of friendship. We've been playing golf together since our early teens, although his interest has never been on the same level as mine. He prefers fishing and cricket, which is why, for his son's third birthday, I gave the little lad some golf clubs. Someone had to rescue him from a life of sporting inadequacy.

We set off on a beautiful, sunny afternoon to play a round of golf that had been festering for a decade. Much has changed in that time. Waterville was founded in 1889, but its rapid rise to fame began on the back of Eddie Hackett's 1973 efforts. His ethos was to let the natural landscape shape the course. In other words, he liked to leave the land as untouched as possible. Carne in County Mayo is the greatest example of this ethos. Waterville was another of his masterpieces, but the Irish-Americans who bought the club in 1987 decided that Waterville's reputation could rise even further. They commissioned the acclaimed golf architect Tom Fazio to upgrade the course.

At the time, I had never heard of Tom Fazio. Who, in their right mind, would ask an American architect famed for his work at Augusta National and Winged Foot to redesign an Irish links? The thinking was bizarre and yet Fazio's work, between 2004 and 2006, has proved a success. Waterville is the most picture-perfect round of golf I have ever played.

There is a final point to make about Waterville, and any golfer worth his salt will know what I'm talking about. Many of America's professionals have come to play Waterville ahead of the Open Championship, but none will be remembered as fondly as Payne Stewart. He was (and still is) universally adored. He loved Waterville and the folks down here loved him back. Indeed, he was honoured with the captaincy of the club in 1999, just weeks before he died so tragically. A bronze statue beside the putting green celebrates the great man, plus fours and all.

In addition to the golf course and Charlie Chaplin, Waterville has other claims to fame. It was here that the first trans-Atlantic cable came ashore. It was laid by Siemens Brothers in 1884, and measured 2,399 nautical miles, stretching from Waterville to Dover Bay in Nova Scotia. It was one of the first and biggest steps in undersea communications and Waterville remained a vital hub for decades. In another communications-related story, there's a famous incident that happened off the coast of Kerry in October 2008. This is the transcript of the radio conversation between the British and the Irish on that day:

> IRISH: Please divert your course 15 degrees to the South, to avoid a collision.

BRITISH: Recommend you divert your course 15 degrees to the North, to avoid a collision.

IRISH: Negative. You will have to divert your course 15 degrees to the South to avoid a collision.

BRITISH: This is the Captain of a British navy ship. I say again, divert YOUR course.

IRISH: Negative. I say again, you will have to divert your course.

BRITISH: THIS IS THE AIRCRAFT CARRIER HMS BRITANNIA, THE SECOND LARGEST SHIP IN THE BRITISH ATLANTIC FLEET. I DEMAND THAT YOU CHANGE YOUR COURSE 15 DEGREES NORTH, I SAY AGAIN, THAT IS 15 DEGREES NORTH, OR COUNTER-MEASURES WILL BE UNDERTAKEN TO ENSURE THE SAFETY OF THIS SHIP.

IRISH: We are a lighthouse. Your call.

Oh sure, this started out as an American tale and I've seen an Australian version, too, but it works so much better in an Irish context. Just picture the lads leaning against the railings under the light, flat caps on, pipes dangling from their mouths, eyes bright with mischief . . .

Charlie's wife had sent him down to me in Kerry for two days of golf, which, by my calculations, meant one night on the town. After Waterville we headed to Killarney, one of Kerry's big tourist attractions.

My dress sense had not improved since my Ballina night-club encounter. If anything, it was worse. On a golf course, dodgy clothing combinations are common, even expected, but in civilised society I was coming to realise that my clothes were regarded as a crime against sighted people.

We walked the town, Charlie's old stomping ground, and found a restaurant that looked suitable for our needs. The maître d' blanched when I entered and he steered us to the back of the restaurant between the loos and the fire exit. I blended right in.

Tatler Jack's pub was a lot less discerning and considerably darker. My yellow shirt had turned a muted beige, matching the sawdust on the floor. I expected traditional Irish music and a few old ones at the bar discussing the demise of Fianna Fáil, or the glory of Kerry's football team, but Tatler Jack's was belting out rock music, the clientele were ordering alco-pops and the girls had decided that displays of heaving bosoms were a national prerequisite. It was National Cleavage Day and I'd missed the memo. We had a couple of pints and left. Charlie had managed to wrangle beds for the night from a friend so we headed back for an early night.

The next day, Charlie led the way to Dooks Golf Club, fifty minutes' drive west of Killarney and on the Ring of Kerry. A friend of mine is a member here and he has always said how good it is. What he never told me about was the scenery. It has the most beautiful surroundings of any golf course in Ireland, which is saying something given the competition from Waterville, Tralee, Narin & Portnoo, Scrabo and County Sligo. Here, there's a 360-degree panorama spread across the Dingle Peninsula, the MacGillycuddy's Reeks, Slieve Mish and the Dingle Mountains. It is easy to see why Kerry is known as The Kingdom.

There were more rounds of golf to be played in and

around the town, and the following morning I arrived at the acclaimed Killarney Golf and Fishing Club. Most people recall the club because of its enchanting setting. Lough Leane embraces the edge of the two old courses (Killeen and Mahony's Point), and across the water the MacGillycuddy's Reeks rise hauntingly above you.

I spent ten minutes on Killeen's 1st hole photographing the landscape and the deer that was thoughtful enough to pose on the water's edge. But for that delay I would have caught Roy and Stella earlier. Instead I encountered the American couple on the 3rd on what is one of the prettiest par threes in the country. They were happy to wait by the green as I played my tee shot and walked up to them.

'Did you see those deer?' Stella enthused. 'Wasn't that wonderful?'

The club's two golf courses have many things going for them and one of those is a large and indifferent population of deer roaming across fairways.

I'd guess that Roy and Stella were in their fifties. He had that portly look of a successful businessman who never had the inclination to exercise. She had that blonde, elegant, ultra thin look that wouldn't look out of place on the back of a Jane Fonda workout DVD. She was also the better golfer by far.

I asked about their trip and was surprised that there were no links courses on the itinerary. American golfers are born with links blood in their veins, and rarely venture away from the coast on visits to Ireland.

Roy, who had yet to say a word other than 'hello', remained mute while his wife explained that links courses would be too difficult for him. Not 'them', but 'him'. Successful businessman he may have been, but clearly of the hen-pecked variety.

They hailed from Boston, and were as enthusiastic as

Americans can be when they return to the country of their ancestors. I asked if I could join them, but Roy looked horrified at the suggestion. Perhaps his golf really was that bad.

I arrived late at Castleisland Golf Club, 25 kilometres from Killarney, and early the following morning I was digging around in bins, like a hobo, trying to find a scorecard I could use. It wasn't the first time I had walked to the tee without a card and it wasn't the last. If I was fortunate to find a card it was usually covered in some nasty rubbish, from mouldy chocolate to sticky, wasp-infested fruit. Occasionally it was covered in a different type of rubbish and, at Castleisland, the scorecard I retrieved from the depths revealed that an unnamed golfer had scored an eight on the 1st, a ten on the 2nd, and a nine on the 3rd. I found the card in the bin by the 4th tee. I guess the card had quit while it was ahead.

Three golf courses qualify as being truly remote in Ireland: Carne, Connemara, and Ceann Sibéal in Dingle. There is something almost otherworldly about driving such a long distance to reach a golf club. Each of the three feels like it's about to fall off the edge of Ireland's west coast. If you're coming to Ireland to enjoy some of our beautiful scenery, then these drives are reason enough to head west, regardless of whether you play golf.

Dingle is some two hours west of Castleisland, and is the most westerly town in Europe. I was driving on the R561 road, which rubs up against the Slieve Mish Mountains on one side and the crystal blue waters of Castlemaine Harbour and Dingle Bay on the other. It eventually merges with the N86, which took me farther along the peninsula and into the small fishing town of Dingle, now better known for its friendly dolphin, Fungi, than its arts, fishing or music.

Tourists thronged the narrow streets and the pretty harbour especially as people clambered on and off boats or stood rooted to the spot with binoculars raised. I parked and went for a wander. I was looking for a coffee shop where I could settle down and play 'guess the tourist', but it was obvious from the dress sense that they were all Americans. Dingle is an interesting little place, where the modern tourism industry grates against the old world existence that many of the locals still cling to. It is a juxtaposition that makes the town all the more intriguing. I blame the dolphin.

It is still a journey from Dingle to the golf course in Ballyferriter. You cross a rural landscape of drystone walls and fields rising into mountains, and when I reached Ireland's most westerly golf course, I almost didn't see it. I looked towards the sea, searching for fluttering flags against a backdrop of crashing waves. But the course is slightly inland, lying beneath the forbidding apron of the Three Sisters – three rocks rising up from a clifftop. The silhouette of Great Blasket Island lingers to the west, but it is the Three Sisters that constantly draw your gaze. The course, by contrast, looks flat and uninspiring from a distance, yet it hides the brilliance of a certain Eddie Hackett. Ceann Sibéal does not have big dunes or acres of space, but it is one of the sterner links tests you will face, thanks in no small part to the burn that crosses eleven holes. It is famous, or perhaps infamous, for the grief it can cause you.

I called in to the clubhouse to ask if I could park the camper overnight.

'We lock the car park at night,' said the woman in the pro shop. 'You'll have to spend the night on the beach.'

'Which beach?' I asked, confused.

'Whichever one you want,' came the reply.

It was a novelty, that's for sure, and down the road I

found a beach all to myself with views of Sybil Head. Black rocks glistened as the tide retreated, birds dipped low over the water and the grass I parked on was so soft, so sandy, that it should have been a golf course.

I sat on the camper van step and watched the sun sink out of sight before driving into nearby Ballyferriter, a small one-street village. I had noticed an attractive pub on the way through and it was to this that I returned. Ó Cathain's Pub was all dark wood and small booths. A long bar was decorated with an assortment of local drinkers and I was surprised by the number of people. There was a gentle hum to the place, a buzz of contentment, and I warmed to it immediately. A couple of nods greeted my approach and I caught the barman's eye. I perched on a stool to reflect on the days gone and the days ahead. My good buddy Finbarr was coming across the country to join me in a couple of days to play the links of Tralee and Ballybunion. Great golf and great company – I could ask for no more.

I ate in the pub, got chatty with a local by the name of Jim, and enjoyed that relaxed, easy atmosphere that sets Irish pubs apart from any other pubs in the world . . . especially those of the Irish-themed variety. Jim wanted to talk about the Kerry football team and I let him. I know nothing about the GAA version of football and prefer hurling by far, but it was nice to have the company and he had a lot of frustration to vent.

I stayed late and then returned to my spot on the beach, Rusty's lights spraying across the soft turf and beach beyond. I checked my emails and one popped up from Finbarr, saying he was looking forward to our round of golf at Tralee the next day. It threw me into a panic. My schedule changed constantly, with each trip being re-written several times as weather or club events affected my plans. I rarely got things wrong but this time I had. Tralee was booked for 1.50 p.m. the following day. There was no way I could tee off with Joe – the gentleman I had met at Skibbereen – at 8.30 a.m., and make it to Tralee Golf Club in time. It was a two-hour drive away. There was only one viable solution.

At 6.45 a.m. the next morning, I teed off in half-light, the Three Sisters at my back, the misty silhouette of Mount Eagle ahead. After the previous evening I was in such a stupor I almost fell into the famous burn on the 1st hole. At least the shock woke me up. I timed the front nine well, and I met Joe back at the clubhouse with my sad story of stupidity. Joe was fine with it and we headed to the par three 10th, behind the clubhouse. He was in his sixties, a solid, white-haired man who plays off a 9 handicap. Anywhere else that would be five or six, because he plays straight and smart golf. He told me the history of the club as we walked around. He was the perfect tour guide, only lacking a hip flask of Irish whiskey, which would have been the perfect hair-of-the-dog for me. The course had been laid out as an eighteen-hole course by Eddie Hackett in the 1970s, but the second nine was completed only twenty years later by Christy O'Connor Junior. Eddie's back nine is the more interesting test as it heads higher, towards the Three Sisters, passing a white horse that should have been confiscated and delivered to Skellig Bay.

There is one final important note to add about Ceann Sibéal, or 'the links at Dingle' as many people call it: it is in the heart of the Gaeltacht, an area where Irish is the first language. As such, the scorecard and the signs in the clubhouse are in Irish (as are the signposts directing you there). They are rightly proud of their Irish heritage and you should listen closely to appreciate the language. Much of Ireland has abandoned our native tongue, so enjoy it when and where you can. Do not fear: they will speak English to you when you need them to. This is not France, where they take a perverse pleasure in making you speak French atrociously before talking back in flawless English.

I rarely had to rush anywhere on my travels. An occasional tee time was almost missed but it was no more than an inconvenience. I often took detours when a sign caught my eye, although not always for the better, as the Healy Pass proved. A missed tee time at Tralee, however, would be more serious because of the course's popularity during the summer. Being a links, and a famous one at that, Americans would be flooding the course. I also had a playing partner driving across from the east coast. My preferred route, over Conor Pass, was dismissed. Those views of Brandon Mountain rising to the west and Kerry Head and Loop Head across the ocean would have to wait for another day.

My rush for Tralee did not have the best of starts. Less than a kilometre from Ceann Sibéal Golf Club, a farmer decided his cows needed their morning walk. I watched them troop out on to the road, a sea of black and white, swaying in slow rhythm as they came towards me. My heart sank. I pulled in as they approached down the narrow road and turned off the engine. Country life is slow and casual, something that should be enjoyed. It calms the soul, just not on that day.

Beyond the cows, coming from Ballyferriter, a Range Rover roared over the hill. The driver had plenty of time to stop but he continued on, only braking at the last minute. Instead of waiting as a normal person would do, he leant on the horn and gesticulated at the farmer to get out of his way. I could see the man's pink jumper but little more. Not that I needed to. The pink jumper meant a golfer was behind the wheel.

To his credit, the farmer hurried his cows along, with the

result that one of them side-swiped Rusty. It was a fair jolt but no one seemed to notice but me.

As the Range Rover crept forward, engine revving louder than was necessary, I spotted the Dublin number plate. Once I could see him clearly, I waved my hands up and down in a universal 'calm down' gesture. He was about my age, with a trimmed black beard. His response was a V sign as he inched past. Maybe if he hadn't caused a cow to clip the camper van, I would have let it go. But he had. I got out of my seat and stepped over to the side door, which I swung open. The Range Rover was right beside me, the driver's window no more than three feet away. I leaned out as the man noticed movement beside him and turned in my direction.

'Wanker!' I roared.

Even the cows turned their heads.

The guy toppled sideways with surprise, his foot slipping off the clutch. The Range Rover stalled, I returned to my seat, turned on the engine and drove off, grinning all the way to Tralee. Country life equals country pace, so deal with it.

Joe's directions helped me to avoid Tralee's claustrophobic town centre and I arrived at one of the world's most beautiful locations for a golf course with time to spare. The golf club sits above Barrow Harbour, a bay of sparkling aquamarine water and beaches that are as golden as they are empty. Banna Strand, below the 15th tee, is where scenes from *Ryan's Daughter* were filmed in 1970. How a movie location scout found this isolated spot (the golf course wasn't here at the time) is beyond me.

After my perfectly timed journey, it turned out that Finbarr had been delayed en route and our tee time was put back, behind three four-balls of Americans. There are few sights more feared on a golf course than Americans with caddies, so we knew we were in for a slow round. Glacial, as it turned out. On the upside, Fin and I got to enjoy Tralee's breathtaking views. It was easy to see why the club is rated as one of the best ocean courses in the world, with several holes vying for the title of Best Hole in Ireland.

Established in 1896, the club moved to its Barrow location in the 1980s when the services of Arnold Palmer were called upon. Tralee produces two types of holes: those produced by Palmer; and those produced by God. So said Arnold Palmer. Whoever was responsible, Tralee is a masterpiece of intrigue and deception, and with the wind up we discovered just how difficult links golf can be. It blew us up and down the dunes, snatched at balls and left us red-faced and raw, like we'd taken to shaving with sandpaper.

After years of wanting to see and play the mighty Ballybunion, one of Ireland's greatest links wasn't ready to reveal her charms just yet. No matter how hard I pushed the camper, the old bucket wasn't going over 90 km/h, and I arrived at Ballybunion after dark.

The clubhouse is an enormous building and not one I'd call elegant. It's fat, squat and angular, but it serves beer and that was fine by me. After ordering a pint from the gorgeous Katie, I struck up a conversation with two other members of the Katie fan club, Americans Bob and Adam. The club's restaurant had just closed, so we asked Katie where we could eat. She made some calls and booked a table for us at the Marina restaurant in the town, while we started discussing the merits of Ireland's different golf courses.

'I've been coming to Ireland for ten years,' Bob said. 'I love the people and I love the links courses. I've played nearly every one of them.' He was a New Yorker, wearing smart logos and looking like a TV commercial. He had that brusque confidence that comes with being a New Yorker.

'So what are your favourite courses?' People had been asking me for my favourites but I was always more interested in what people pick as their best.

True to form, there was little hesitation from Bob.

'Royal County Down, Waterville, Ballybunion and The Island.' He snapped them off in quick succession.

'And what about you, Adam?'

'Ballybunion,' he said, shrugging sheepishly.

I waited for more, but he wasn't forthcoming.

Bob was laughing. 'It's his first trip, and today was his first round of links golf.'

By the time Fin arrived, after a visit to nearby family, we were so deep into the reasons why The Island is better than Portmarnock that any non-golfer would have been put to sleep. As we headed for the restaurant, we tried to thank Katie for her help but she was curled up on the floor, snoring.

It took five minutes to discover what a small world it is. Fin asked the guys where in New York they were from and where they played golf. Bob listed a golf club where one of Fin's close friends is a member. Bob knew him.

The guys had played Ballybunion that day and were heading to Tralee in the morning, so the opposite of our plans. We swapped stories and advice but Fin and I gave up at midnight, deciding we needed sleep if we were to do Ballybunion justice.

The next morning was what you might call a quilted day: the sun was up there, but it broke through the ridges of thin clouds only occasionally. I was having breakfast in the clubhouse before Finbarr arrived from his hotel. We chatted briefly as he tried to catch the eye of the woman who'd served me. He was after a coffee.

'You won't have much luck there,' I said. 'Couldn't even get a smile out of her.'

Finbarr looked surprised. My next words were not well chosen. 'I bet you a pint you can't get her to smile.'

A grin slid across his face and he was up out of his seat and striding towards her before I could slap myself for being so dumb.

Seconds later the woman was smiling and giggling like a teenager. I shook my head in despair. Fin is a charmer.

When he returned, he slipped a piece of paper onto the table and pushed it towards me.

'What's this?'

He grinned again. 'Laura's telephone number.'

I let out a sigh and rolled my eyes. 'You're married,' I reminded him.

'Hey, it's not for me. You're the one staying tonight.' He gave me a condescending pat on the shoulder. 'You might need it, although I doubt she'll be impressed by that camper van of yours.'

And with that we headed out to do battle with the great links of Ballybunion.

Fin's words on the 1st tee, however, were not what I was expecting.

'A mobile home park! Seriously.'

Our opening tee shot was straight at a smorgasbord of mobile homes, scattered around like Lego. Not exactly appetising. Then again, Ballybunion was established in 1893, long before these monstrosities arrived. The cemetery to the right of the fairway has, I imagine, been there a lot longer and it adds a quirky touch.

There is a halfway house by the 6th tee and I could hear Finbarr's stomach rumbling from yards away. The coffee had woken him up and now he needed feeding. We popped in for a bacon and sausage roll and came out with a lot more.

Fin discovered two brand new friends as he walked back to his bag. Two dogs had appeared from nowhere and nuzzled up to him in the hope of scraps. We avoided their mournful eyes and enthusiastic tails, but it's not the dogs you have to worry about. No, it's the crows. In these parts they have learned a thing or two about scavenging for food. You can buy a chocolate bar and put it in your bag, but if you walk away to play a shot don't expect it to be there when you get back. The crows can overcome zips and flaps to get what they're after. Perhaps that's why you get a second chance to visit the same halfway house at the 9th.

Ballybunion's big dunes can swallow you whole so, when we reached the 11th tee, I hung my head in despair as Finbarr had to go and open his big mouth.

I have always believed in the power of negative positivity. When you play your golf at Greystones it is something that comes naturally. After you walk off the 9th there's a two-minute walk to the back nine, during which time you are going through hell or burning with endless optimism. Two minutes is too long to dwell on how well or how badly you are playing, because the power of negative positivity means that whatever you tell yourself it isn't going to work. Consider the number of times you've stood on the 18th and said: 'All I have to do is par/bogey/birdie/not screw up the last hole and I can win this.' Or how about: 'I won't three putt from here'? I'm sure Bob Rotella would have a much more catchy and enlightening term for it, but I call it negative positivity. Everybody else calls it the Kiss of Death.

And Finbarr had uttered the most classic words of all: 'I haven't lost a ball.'

Indeed, his game had been superb, firing freely at greens and sinking a few tricky putts, but he didn't even have the decency to end his statement with the word 'yet'. Fin plays off an 18 handicap, although he is considerably better than that. He should know better, especially when we were about to play one of the best holes in the world, down through the dunes, high above the beach.

Sure enough, Fin hit his drive and we watched as it faded on the wind and soared out to sea. A couple was walking on the sand, tossing a ball into the water for their dog, and Fin's ball splashed down well beyond them. The couple didn't notice but the dog did, leaping through the water and paddling like mad as his owners roared at him to come back.

Fin teed up again and didn't alarm the dog this time, but the ball was never seen again. On the next tee I chastised him for his foolishness.

'You never verbalise such things,' I said in my most patronising tone. 'That's like me saying I haven't had a double bogey.' Naturally, I double bogeyed the 12th to ruin a good score card, but at least I'd made my point, and Fin's mood improved dramatically.

Irish golf is full of characters: from the oddball professionals to the enthusiastic general managers to the hard-working greenkeepers. But nothing is as entertaining as the golfers themselves. I was playing Ballybunion's 13th and pulled my drive into the left-hand rough. Fin and I parted ways as I went off to search for the ball. I reached the top of a low dune and the wind blew voices towards me from the 2nd fairway, words snapping in the breeze.

'How far is it, Seanie?'

I glanced across. Standing knee high in marram grasses was an American golfer and her caddie. She was dressed impeccably as she eyed the distant green on the dune top.

Seanie, an older lad wearing a dark woollen jumper, peered towards the green momentarily and then back at the fairway.

'You've got 140 yards to the green; 150 to the pin,' he replied calmly.

She nodded her head and turned her face to the wind, her blonde ponytail flapping out of the hole in her baseball cap. 'A 4 iron,' she said emphatically.

Seanie opened his mouth, changed his mind, and handed over the requested club. As she set herself up for the shot, he glanced up at me and shrugged, knowing he had a long day ahead.

The swing was slow and rather elegant . . . but completely ineffective through the thick Ballybunion rough. She made contact at least, and the ball bumbled through the grass.

Seanie looked up at the green with eyes that had seen it all before and reached for his golfer's club.

'You've got 135 yards to the green; 145 to the pin,' he said, with not even a hint of mischief.

I have played a number of courses with Fin over the years, including Royals County Down, Portrush and Dublin, Portstewart, Tralee, The European, Gleneagles, Wentworth, Hoylake and Carnoustie, and I know he has played the likes of Kingsbarns, Royal Birkdale and several other 'big' courses. So when he said that Ballybunion Old is the best of them all, I know he's speaking from experience. We walked off the 18th, sated and overawed by the course. Ballybunion was all I'd hoped it would be and there was another 18 to come.

I suppose it was inevitable. Driving around, playing golf day in, day out. At some point I was bound to encounter a priest. On the Ballybunion Cashen course I got a double helping. Jack and John were two local priests who found themselves in the pleasant position of playing some exceptional links golf when the good Lord allowed. We met them on the 3rd hole and joined forces owing to the slow pace of play ahead.

'I know your grandmother's sister,' John quipped to Finbarr after introductions were made.

It wasn't even a joke, just further proof that it's a small world. One side of Finbarr's family is from nearby Ardfert, and John knew them.

And from that point on, no matter how hard he tried, Finbarr managed to take the Lord's name in vain on every bad shot. He'd apologise, of course. Until the next bad shot. Fin simply doesn't do swearing or tantrums, but I had to close my eyes to avoid watching my friend continually confound himself with his sudden blaspheming yips. Jack and John didn't seem to be fussed. I imagine they've heard far worse.

It was a hot day – we had been blessed – and it took us two hours and forty-five minutes to complete nine holes. Jack and John had had enough and Finbarr needed to head back to Rosslare, so we agreed to retire. In the clubhouse we heard that the delay was due to five groups of golfers from Turkey, including the Professional from Istanbul Golf Club. With the diaspora settling on every corner of the planet, it came as no surprise to discover the Pro's mother came from Ballybunion. The Irish have made the planet a very small place indeed.

I hung around in the bar until 6 p.m., before heading to the 10th tee to play on one of those gloriously sunny and mellow evenings. The light turned the sand to gold and the grasses to a rich, shimmering green. I had the course to myself and I took my time on nine magnificent holes that rival any on the island. My shadow, my only companion, matched my stride or leapt into the dunes as I passed. The putts rolled in, the sound of the ocean filled my ears and my shoulders were so relaxed I could have slipped them off and tucked them into my bag. It's at times like these that you realise how lucky you are.

The famous market town of Listowel lies halfway between Ballybunion and Ardagh, my next stop. Listowel Writers' Week started in 1971, and the town is now considered to be the literary capital of Ireland . . . by the townspeople anyway. I had missed the festival by a couple of weeks and my drive through its streets at first light revealed nothing of literary worthiness, only the outline of its fifteenth-century castle.

Newcastle West Golf Club was the trigger for my book *Hooked*, a course that no one at my home club knew anything about and failed to make any directory on Irish golf that I could find. The club was founded in 1938, and moved to its current location in 1994. Evidently, they like to keep their club a private affair, hidden away from prying eyes and interested golfers. With no signposts to follow, I drove down tree-lined lanes, past farms, double-backing on myself thanks to nifty ten-point turns in the smallest gateways that man has ever created, until I arrived at the club entrance through sheer luck.

Many other clubs pursue a similar policy of invisibility and there is an element of Irishness to it. The Irish, you see, like you to get lost like no one else . . . only then can we outwit you with classics one-liners such as: 'You want to get to Athlone? Sure, I wouldn't start from here' or, upon being questioned about the lack of signposts, 'Sure, why would we need them? We know where we're going.' It leaves tourists mystified whenever they venture off the beaten path. That or in fits of screaming rage.

Limerick Golf Club, 40 kilometres east, dates back to 1891, and it was teeming with golfers. Slow golfers as it turned out, thanks to a society outing. Twice I had the opportunity to lie under a tree and catch a quick nap. Turned out I was going to need the energy.

When I got back to the car park I discovered a flat tyre. Rusty was slumped on its back haunches, looking dejected. As I was about to discover, a twenty-year-old camper van with a flat requires a lot of manual labour. You attach the small handle to the jack and turn it 180 degrees. Then you ratchet it back and repeat. It took twenty minutes to hoist Rusty to the necessary height, by which stage I was drenched in sweat, swearing loudly and bleeding from several scraped knuckles.

Once I had the van high enough to remove the wheel I felt I'd achieved a victory. I slapped on the spare tyre, tightened the bolts and lowered the jack . . . and then watched as the camper slowly slumped back to the same position as the spare went flat, too.

I called a taxi. The taxi came. I loaded the flat tyre into his boot and he drove me to a garage. The air hose had been stolen. It had been stolen at the next garage too. Kids, apparently. Why, I don't know. They were too young for enemas. Then again, who knows what kind of things kids are into these days. The third garage had what I needed and I filled the tyre with air. It was dark by the time I returned, so I replaced the tyre in the glow of the clubhouse lights and then went for my third and much needed shower of the day, dirty, exhausted and bloody fed up.

I needed a pint and the impressive clubhouse, with its white walls and elegant carpet was a touch more luxurious than most clubhouses I had visited. I walked up the stairs and into a bar full of noise. The society outing was going strong and my arrival coincided with the prize-giving. The group of about sixty golfers had been wined and dined and were getting somewhat raucous as the man in charge tried to make a speech. Judging by the catcalls, his name was Mick, and would he please get a-feckin move on.

He was kitted out in suit and tie and took his duties seriously, flapping his hands at people to calm them down. I slipped away to the bar and then watched the proceedings with a cool pint in hand. A round of somewhat bored applause followed Mick's mercifully short speech before he shuffled his cards and started announcing prizes. There were plenty of them too, including a nearest-the-pin on one of the par threes. It was won by one of the ladies.

'Mary O'Sullivan wins nearest-the-pin, with a distance to the hole of two feet,' Mick announced to a surprised audience. 'Congratulations, Mary.'

A sizeable woman in her fifties got up and shuffled across to Mick with a smile so wide it must have hurt. She was flushed with embarrassment and quickly shuffled back to the safety of her seat after collecting her prize. Her friends leaned in and congratulated her as the prize-giving continued.

The woman looked delighted and shocked in equal measure, and after the prize-giving was over and people started to depart, I found myself beside her at the bar.

'Well done,' I said. 'You must be chuffed.'

'Oh I am. I've never won anything in my life. I can't believe it, you know. My husband's not going to believe this.' The words gushed out.

'What club did you hit?' I enquired.

She thought about it for a second, clearly reliving the moment. 'It was my 3 wood,' she said, 'and then a pitching wedge for my second shot.'

I opened my mouth, and then decided there was not a lot I could say without ruining her evening. The requirement of taking only one shot in a nearest-the-pin competition was clearly lost on her . . . and her playing partners.

The air in the spare tyre was sufficient to get me to a garage the next day and I sat in a café across the road as both tyres were repaired. As I got back on the road I felt this huge wave of relief wash over me. I don't know why. There was a sense that I had avoided total disaster, and yet this was nowhere near as bad as the water tank bursting in Birr.

A couple of years back I watched a programme made by Peter Cox, an Irish photographer, who had taken some non-celebrity celebrity under his wing to introduce said celebrity to the joys of photography. They visited Lough Gur, a short distance south of Limerick City, and the Grange Stone Circle. It is Ireland's largest, measuring 150 feet in diameter with 113 stones.

Many of Ireland's stone circles lie on raised hillsides, exposed to the elements and the power of nature. Lough Gur is not one of those. Here there are trees and an orderliness that seems at odds with its 2000BC formation. You might be tempted to have a picnic on the soft grass.

I followed the narrow, uneven path under the trees towards the muscular entrance stones. If there was a sense of eeriness about something so old and mystical, it was quickly quashed by a large Englishman in a bright green tracksuit. I stepped between the stones and was almost flattened as he ran past, encircling the perimeter.

'Awright mate, sorry about that,' he shouted over his shoulder, barely breaking stride.

I climbed to my feet and was almost flattened by another, mercifully smaller, individual. Another followed and then another. There were four in all – a father and three teenage boys – racing around the stone circle like it was the Olympics. At least they were appropriately dressed, their hideously matching nylon tracksuits creating enough static to power a small country.

The father reached the entrance stones first and threw his arms high in celebration, letting out a whoop of victory. The three boys arrived behind and immediately started a scuffle over alleged cheating. Dad waded in and broke it up. With all that static electricity I was surprised someone didn't spontaneously combust or at least electrocute one of the others.

'Sorry, mate,' the father repeated, with a strong east London twang. 'Having a bit of a laugh, awright.' He turned to the three bickering siblings. 'Shut it you lot,' he snapped in a tone that brought instant silence.

He walked over to me in that cocky kind of way, and I noted his size for the first time. Not tall, but broad across the shoulders and muscles bulging through the nylon. If I'd arrived a bit later he'd probably have been shot-putting the four tonne stones for his second event.

'Love the place,' he said. 'Bet the Irish builders put these in a few years back. Am I right?'

I had no idea if he was joking or not so I stayed silent.

'Probably something to do with *Father Ted* and one of Dougal's mad schemes. Am I right?'

Same question. If I didn't say something soon he'd think I was a moron.

'Ah go on, go on, go on,' I managed.

He cracked up, then roared at the boys. They marched off down the path, leaving me with the stones and the Fey who had been in hiding for the last quarter of an hour.

Father Ted, as an English friend once noted after a visit to County Cavan, is not a comedy but a documentary. Based on my recent encounter, so is *EastEnders*.

We confuse visiting golfers in a number of ways in this country. First there are the roads and their lack of signs, the different names for the same place and that sense of despair when your odometer tells you that you're 5 kilometres nearer to a place but a sign at a crossroads says that you're 2 kilometres farther away . . . and yet you're going in the right direction. The second reason is one reserved especially for golfers, and that's when two golf courses choose the same name. There are two Portmarnocks in Dublin, and there are two Adares in, well, Adare. On the outskirts of one of Ireland's quaintest villages, replete with thatched cottages and sparkling whitewashed walls, there are two golf clubs, one named Adare Golf Club and the other Adare Manor Golf Club. They are separated by nothing more than a single word and 20 yards of pathway that could see someone walk off Adare's 14th green and onto Adare Manor's 3rd. You might think that the names are distinctive enough but that only compounds the underlying confusion. Adare Manor, the Neo-Gothic manor built in the 1800s and now home to a five-star hotel, is in the grounds of Adare Golf Club, and not Adare Manor Golf Club. Adare Golf Club, thanks to having the hotel on its premises, also refers to itself as Adare Manor Resort. Are you still with me? Imagine how golfers must feel when they arrive to play Ireland's best parkland and discover a charmingly odd, tight par sixty-nine instead!

There are long and complicated stories about the naming of the clubs, but Adare Manor Golf Club was founded in 1900, while the glamorous Adare Golf Club opened in 1995 and has hosted the Irish Open twice – Richard Finch famously falling in the water on the final hole in 2008. He still won.

My arrival was anything but glamorous. I stopped at Adare's security hut off the N21 road, and got that sinking feeling as rain started to fall. I jumped down from the camper van as the security guard came out of his hut, staring in horror at Rusty.

'Who are you?' he asked curtly, his clipboard in hand.

I was staring at the wheel in disbelief as I gave him my name, ignoring the rain. A different tyre, another flat.

The bulky security guard looked at where I was staring. 'You've got a puncture,' he said, an edge of joyful malice in his voice.

I noticed the parking area beside the hut. I'll fix it there, I thought. I won't be in anyone's way.

But the security guard was having none of it. He went off to verify my authenticity and when he came back he read my mind. 'You'll have to move. Drive up to the clubhouse. You can't block the entrance.'

His generosity knew no bounds.

The clubhouse was considerably farther away than I'd thought, along an avenue of tall trees. I drove slowly, but as a connoisseur of punctures at this stage, I had a good idea what was happening. Or maybe it was the sound of grating metal and flying sparks that alerted me to my plight. By the time I rolled to a stop, the rain was lashing, my tyre was shredded and my anger had reached boiling point.

I stomped into the clubhouse. The last thing I needed was for someone to be nice to me, but that's exactly what I got. The girl in the golf shop was as nice as pie.

'Welcome, Mr Markham, yes, Mr Markham. A puncture? Oh how horrid, Mr Markham.'

She dished out a scorecard and strokesaver and sent me off to the tee with a sweet smile. I couldn't stay mad for long under the gaze of a gorgeous Irish lass like that.

Things improved on the 1st tee, too. True, they weren't as attractive as the girl I'd left behind, but Tommy, Jamie and Ian had something else going for them: they were Scottish and they had buggies. They invited me to join them and in light of the intense downpour I accepted willingly.

'I'll take that,' said Pat, the Starter, reaching for my trolley. 'I'll leave it up by the pro shop.'

'Thanks. By any chance do you know anyone who can help me with a flat tyre?' My knuckles were still a mountain range of scabs and I was happy to pay someone to do the hard labour for me.

'I'll get the pro shop to call Tom for you. He's a local lad. He'll have it done right quick.' Pat was already heading back the way I'd come, my cheap trolley dancing around behind him.

All that great customer service had quelled my rage and I stepped onto the 1st tee in a completely new frame of mind.

The three Scots were members at West Kilbride Golf Club, 20 miles from Royal Troon on the west coast.

When a Scotsman says 'aye' you can't help but smile. It's like a nod, a wink and a confirmation all wrapped up in one, with a cheeky accent that suggests they know something you don't. And the Scots say 'aye' a lot.

The talk seemed to focus on two things: Irish golf courses versus their Scottish cousins, and drink. And when I say drink I mean the merits of Guinness, which the boys had enjoyed bountifully, and the whole debate of Irish whiskey versus Scotch whisky.

I knew Irish whiskey was better because it had been an important part of my school education.

'Why is Irish whiskey spelt with an "e"?' Mr Lush, my old geography teacher would ask, never fully appreciating the irony of his name. 'Because the e is for "everything".'

'Are you over to play any of the links?' I enquired of Tommy as we zipped up the 1st fairway.

'Not at all,' he laughed from under a floppy waterproof hat that flipped up and down with the buggy's motion. 'Why would we when we have the best links in the world on our side of the water?'

Combined, Ireland and Scotland have a rather large share of the world's links courses – plenty for everyone – so why argue about who has the best. Besides, there were three of them and only one of me.

'One of our friends works here, so we came over to visit and play the course. We played yesterday too. Aye, in better weather than this.'

Despite the weather, the three Scots were in fine form. Let's be honest, if there's one place where it rains more than Ireland, it's Scotland. And by the 10th hole, the sun had come out and four men stepped out of dripping waterproofs and quietly and joyfully steamed in the sunshine.

I fell completely under Adare's spell. It is a beautiful place, one that would be beautiful with or without the golf course. I had so much fun that I forgot about the security guard and I forgot about my flat tyre. By the time I got back to the camper I was already an hour late for my next tee time . . . and Tom, the puncture-repair man, wasn't about. So it was down on my knees again, grovelling at Rusty's underbelly as I slowly cranked her up. Adare is far too refined a place for people to walk past making smart comments, but that may have had something to do with the cursing that was coming out of my mouth.

My good mood had pretty much evaporated as I headed for Castletroy, making a detour to buy a new tyre for €80 on the way.

But once again I encountered some fun-loving golfers who snapped me out of it. Donal, Kevin and Rory were in their mid-teens, an entertaining and bickering trio who knew how to push each other's buttons. From 'minging' girlfriends to dodgy haircuts, anything was fair game.

Donal watched me making notes on the course.

'Are you writing a book or something?' he asked.

The other two stopped in their tracks.

'Yep,' I replied, cautiously.

'What's it called?'

'*Hooked.*'

There were some moments of silence as the three amigos exchanged glances and from then on they were determined to get themselves mentioned, telling me their most outrageous stories and their greatest deeds. I couldn't write it down fast enough and some of it is unprintable.

Rory told me that the built-like-a-bull Kevin had just won a Senior School's Rugby medal with Castletroy School. He was only in fourth year, so the school would have him for another two years. Who knows, we may see him in later years playing for the mighty Munster. Donal was tall, slight and blond, and knocked the ball serious distances. He was a leftie too, and had the most outrageous handicap I'd heard of. He had birdie putts aplenty and then chipped in for a birdie on 16. 'Put that in your book,' he said smugly. All that and a handicap of 15 . . . from Lahinch no less.

Lahinch was a few days away and there was a lot of golf, travel and disgusted children to come before then. And what I thought was a near-death experience.

In the previous weeks I'd had punctures, a burst water tank, a leaking roof and a dislocated bumper, so when the camper van started to rattle and shake at 6.03 a.m., I thought it was in its death throes. The vibrations reached a crescendo and I flung myself from the bed, out the side door and onto wet grass . . . and then watched as a plane roared overhead. It was the first flight of the day from Shannon Airport and the word 'Ryanair' glared down at me.

'Bastards,' I yelled, shaking a fist, which is what so many people shout when they see the word 'Ryanair'.

I was wide awake – and wet – so I embarked on one of the earliest tee times of my travels. I was exhausted before I started, but I knew that I had a real bed to look forward to that night.

Once or twice on my journey, I found friends who were willing to accommodate me for a night or two. Some I had just made, such as Tony Brady at Ballinlough Castle, while others dated back to university and beyond. I know that many people have been envious of the journey I made and the courses I played, but it wasn't always plain sailing. There were difficulties along the way and loneliness was one of the worst, so settling down with friends for a night was a rare and much appreciated treat.

Mark and Christine offered me a bed for a couple of nights. They lived in Ennis, County Clare, thirty minutes north of Shannon, on one of those big, winding estates with sufficient space to house three children and a wandering golfer.

My arrival was greeted by a lot of screaming. Kids ran amok and a barbecue sizzled away. A sizeable gang of neighbours was tucking in to one of Mark's famous barbecues and I barely had time to say hello before a burger was stuck in one hand and a beer in the other. Christine pulled me away a while later and showed me my room, before demanding a tour of the camper van. Between exiting the front door and reaching the camper I acquired a flotilla of six children behind Christine.

I led the way, like the Pied Piper of Hamelin, and we all clambered in. Frank, who was Mark and Christine's youngest, headed straight for the steering wheel and took us away on some fantasy journey involving a lot of screeching brakes and sharp turns. The girls were reluctant to touch anything.

'What is it, Roisin?' Christine asked a little girl in a light yellow dress.

'Where do you sleep?' Roisin asked, looking for a bed. She was no more than six.

I pointed at the bed, stowed away tight to the ceiling. 'Up there.'

She looked at the bed, looked back at me with sweet, innocent blue eyes and then down at my belly. 'How do you fit?'

I thought Christine was going to wet herself.

An older girl stepped forward.

'Is this where you live?' she asked hesitantly, a deep furrow between her eyebrows.

'Yes,' I said, trying to ignore the tears pouring down Christine's face and the girl's tone of incredulity.

The little girl's face screwed up in horror. 'That's disgusting,' she managed to splutter before escaping from the camper van faster than I had the previous day.

There's nothing quite like a child to put you in your place.

After two days of home cooking, sinking into a deep armchair with a few beers and chatting to friends, I turned the camper for Kilrush and Kilkee on the County Clare coastline. I drove alongside the mighty River Shannon, through Labasheeda and around Clonderalaw Bay. Soon afterwards, as the road trickled close to the water's edge, Scattery Island appeared directly ahead. It is a small island with a mix of history. There is a sixth-century monastery, a 300-metre-high round tower and the remains of a gun rampart from the Napoleonic Wars. Interesting times.

The road led on through Kilrush and out towards Kilkee town. Kilkee Golf Cub sits on the ocean's edge with dramatic

Atlantic views and a clifftop hole that could be terrifying on a windy day. It is playfully called the Pebble Beach of the West, a mild embellishment but one that does the club no harm, judging by the eagerness of some Swedes I had met in Shannon who were keen to play here. I joined up with Ned, Sammy and Tony for the last few holes, and then accepted their invitation to join them at Scott's Bar, a famous Kilkee watering hole. We sat outside, enjoying the late afternoon sun as I learned that Sammy ran a bar in Brooklyn. He was home for a few days, catching up with friends, and Scott's was his local. He hadn't lost his Clare accent, which must have gone down a treat in Brooklyn. A drink became two and the discussion moved to rugby.

'I was at the game, you know,' Ned chirped up.

There was a lengthy pause from all present.

'The game?' I asked.

'He means the Game.' Tony gave me a serious nod.

I felt the cynic in me coming out. 'You were at the Game? Really?'

Ned took a drink. 'Yep. Got the ticket to prove it.'

The game he was referring to was the famous match in 1978, when Munster beat the All Blacks 12-0. It remains a historic moment in Irish rugby, which is why something in the region of 150,000 people claim to have been at Thomond Park, despite the ground's capacity being only 8,000. Legend, folklore, fairytale, and it has been summed up perfectly in a play entitled *Alone It Stands*.

It was threatening to become a session when the guys saw sense and headed their own ways.

I strolled back up O'Curry Street, and down onto the strand. It was dark and peaceful walking along the curve of Moore Bay, the town on my right, sea and sand on my left. It's a small town and I passed not another soul as I returned to the clubhouse car park ten minutes away. I was a touch dizzy but not concerned as the following day was a day off.

The two priests I'd played with at Ballybunion had pointed across the sea, where the Shannon greeted the Atlantic Ocean, and told me about a beautiful place called Loop Head.

'As quiet as the grave,' one of them had said.

That was my destination as I drove from Kilkee down the peninsula, past Castle Point and Rinevilla Bay. The small village of Kilbaha is almost at the tip, and once you see the lighthouse, standing tall, white and proud on the clifftops, you know you're almost there. It was not an interesting drive, the landscape being too flat, but Loop Head more than made up for it.

This is where Ireland's biggest and longest river empties into the Atlantic. The Shannon is over 220 miles long and it divides the east of Ireland from the west. Some in the west are delighted by such a proposition but the Shannon is a vitally important waterway to the entire nation of Ireland, economically, culturally and historically. I crossed it on several occasions and I felt it was fitting that I now got to see where river became ocean.

As a child, I was taken to many of Ireland's renowned tourist destinations: the Giant's Causeway, Connemara, The Burren and the Cliffs of Moher chief among them. There are many other places that don't enjoy the kissing-the-blarney-stone-searching-for-leprechauns tourism hype and, without the hordes of tourists, it makes these sights all the more beautiful. The cliffs of Slieve League in County Donegal are one such example; Loop Head is another.

I parked and set off towards the lighthouse. The cliffs run northeast along the coastline, until all you can see are distant headlands. Next to the lighthouse a giant hunk of rock is planted in the sea, 100 metres high and no more than a fatal leap across the void. From some angles this dramatic sea stack, known as Diarmuid and Grainne's Rock after the star-crossed lovers of Irish mythology, looks like a badly parked truck; from others, it resembles an elephant's rear end. With its myriad of rock layers it is home to thousands of birds that breed here. I sat and watched them for over an hour as they swooped down towards the most perfect green water that thunders against the base and explodes into white. The way the ocean retreated, like a child drawing breath to blow out candles, brought out goosebumps. The sound was terrifying, even more so from the rocky ledge I found on one clifftop.

The black stone radiated warmth as I lay down and inched forward until I was staring straight down at the ocean. The swell of the sea was hypnotic and the roar of the bursting waves vibrated against my face. This area is well known for its petrels, choughs, rosefinch and a variety of gulls. I knew not which I was looking at, but the birds danced on the wind like puppets on a string, the wind snapping at them as the air currents turned them into darts of light. They came close enough to touch.

It is ironic, is it not, that in order to 'go on holiday' so many of us need to step onto a plane, cross an ocean, seek out the sun, all the while ignoring the beauty of our homeland. How often when friends visit from abroad do we recommend places to go that we've never been to ourselves, even those nearby? Sure, we say, we could visit them any time, and yet we never do.

I ate lunch outside, sitting on soft, springy turf, with views up the coastline. Whales pass this way, as do the occasional tourists, but I had the spot to myself. There is something magical about finding a slice of heaven and having it all to yourself, feeling Ireland's beauty soak through your feet and fill your soul.

I drove back to Kilkee and then 10 kilometres to the north, to the scene of one of Ireland's great evolutionary clashes. In the 1990s, the rarely sighted Great White Shark fought the even rarer Vertigo Angustior. In the dunes along Doughmore Bay they fought, battling for the high ground and the hearts and minds of the golfing world. Measuring a mere 1.8mm long, the Vertigo Angustior finally won out, forcing Greg Norman to weave the wonders of Doonbeg around the dunes that were one of the last habitats of these tiny snails.

'Ridiculous,' one of my playing partners said to me at the time. 'Why should a snail that size get in the way of a golf course?'

Because, I wanted to reply, mankind is already wiping out species all over the planet for the craziest reasons and a golf course is irrelevant in the grand scheme of things. Who are we to dictate why the size of a creature makes it irrelevant? It's all part of the food chain, part of evolution and part of the reason why we have risen to the top of that food chain.

Instead I called him a fecking eejit, and we moved on.

When it came down to it, Greg Norman never really stood a chance. The environment won. As a result, the Doonbeg golf links had to avoid some magnificent dunes in the centre of the course. Perhaps this was a loss for the course, but what Norman left behind is a testament to skill and excitement that befits the Great White Shark himself. And a thriving snail population.

The drive to Doonbeg was much like Ballyliffin. Out of a flat landscape a building rises into view, growing ever more prominent. I spotted The Lodge shortly after leaving Doonbeg village on the N67. The Lodge and its many cottages practically make up their own village in this American-style resort, sitting by the sea and exuding luxury and class.

From Waterville to Sligo, there are six links courses dating back to the nineteenth century: Waterville, Dooks, Tralee (albeit in a new location), Ballybunion, Lahinch and County Sligo Golf Club. Each can claim to be among the best in the world, so when the upstart Doonbeg arrived it had one hell of a reputation to live up to. That it has achieved praise and awards in equal measure is proof of the imagination of Greg Norman.

And with its luxury overtones I was not surprised to be exiled to a small car park. My home for the night was halfway along the long entrance road, where a small spit of black tarmac had been dropped into the middle of sand and reeds. It looked like it was floating. I parked as the day ended, not far from a battered, yellow VW camper. It was old school, with a yellow bottom, white top and the spare tyre poised on the front. I had seriously considered one of these for my travels, so I did a tour and reminded myself that I had made the right decision. Too small, no bathroom and always having to bend in half to move about . . . which meant no way to practice my putting.

I sat down on Rusty's outside step with a bottle of beer beside me. It was ice cold, almost frozen, and I chilled out while I waited for it to thaw. A movement in the dunes distracted me. Two men appeared carrying surfboards. Kitted out in wet suits, they had their gear pulled down to their waist. More surfer types I could not imagine. Scrawny, long hair and so laid back their heads were practically bouncing on the sand.

They looked my way and said hello as they strapped their boards to the roof and began analysing the waves Doughmore Bay had thrown their way. It was the rasp of my beer bottle opening that caught their attention. Pretty soon after that there were three open beers and the lads were sitting on deckchairs retrieved from the VW.

Thierry was utterly relaxed, in that gloriously French way. Who needs to say words when you can say it with a Gallic shrug! Ray was from England. A couple of sentences and I'd nailed his Brummie accent. In his late twenties and of a similar age to Thierry, he had dozens of tiny scars down his arms and legs. When he caught me looking, he shrugged and said 'Florida', as if that explained everything.

'This,' said Thierry gesturing at my camper van, 'is the way to travel.' His voice was deep and lazy and he held onto words so long that most Irish folk would have completed another sentence in the time. He stood up and took a closer look. Hands on hips, he nodded to himself as he peered inside.

'Imagine,' he said, turning to Ray, 'if we travel with the boards on the inside. You surf?' he asked me.

I looked at Thierry and Ray, both whippet thin, tightly muscled in short wetsuits, long hair falling around their faces and bearing a skin colour that resembled well-worn leather. Then I considered how I looked in my V-neck golf sweater and sensible golfing trousers.

'No,' I replied. 'I golf.'

Thierry made a face and followed it with another glorious hitch of the shoulders. 'Dud,' he muttered.

Golf barely came in to the conversation as more beers were drunk and we watched the sun disappear behind the dunes. Mostly we talked about Thierry's annual pilgrimage, which started in Portugal, came up through France and finished in Ireland and England . . . before he headed back to Portugal and started all over again. It was such a different lifestyle to anything I knew. He worked from time to time, doing painting and manual labour to raise the money for travel costs and food, although judging by the ribcage on display he ate little.

I learned a lot of surfing terminology, like 'pumping', 'carving' and 'pearl'. Apparently I was a 'kook', which meant I was a wannabe surfer with few necessary skills. I disagreed: I had no skills whatsoever. I once tried surfing in Australia and couldn't stand up straight without falling over. Not a promising start when the board's still lying on the beach.

Ray wasn't impressed by the Doonbeg Resort that interfered with what he saw as a surfer's entitlement to good waves. 'What is a "right of way"?' he asked at one point.

The shadows were fading from the grasses and the guys began packing up.

'Where next?' I asked.

'Strandhill,' Ray replied, handing his empty bottles to Thierry.

I laughed. 'You'll find another golf course right next to the beach.'

Thierry nodded. 'I have been before.' He handed me the bottles. 'You recycle, yes?'

I took the bottles and he slapped me on the shoulder and pointed a finger at me. 'You try surfing,' he said and then slapped his belly as he looked at mine. 'It's never too late, dud.' He picked up his chair and headed over to the VW.

Ray held his deckchair in one hand and offered me the other. 'Ta for the beers.' Then he started laughing. 'Man, you should have seen your face when he called you "dud". Classic. He was calling you "dude".'

Arms hanging out of windows, boards strapped to the roof, they left the way I had come.

From the newness and novelty of Doonbeg to the old and traditional refinement of Lahinch, barely a day separated me from two of the grandest golf courses in Ireland. Lahinch lay to the north but there were two places I wanted to visit along the way.

First came Spanish Point, named after the unfortunate Spanish sailors who died here in 1588, when the Spanish

Armada's *San Marcos* and *San Esteban* foundered in storms. Those who didn't drown and made it to land had nothing to celebrate for they were either slaughtered on the beach or captured by Boethius Clancy and held at his nearby castle. From there they were taken to *Cnoc na Crocaire* where they were hanged. The bodies were thrown in a mass grave known as *Tuama na Spaineach*, and so Spanish Point was born.

There's a nine-hole golf course, too, but that plays a less significant part in Spanish Point's story. History suggests that the Spaniards' clubs went down with the ships.

Twenty-five kilometres farther on, and beyond Lahinch, the towering Cliffs of Moher remain one of Ireland's top tourist attractions. I wasn't playing Lahinch until the following day, so I drove straight through the village and out to the visitor centre, which opened in 2007. It has been squeezed into the hillside to create minimal visual impact, and it was like walking into a cave – albeit one with the latest mod-cons. I wandered around the centre briefly but, like most visitors, what I was after was the sight of the towering cliffs and that sense of immense power.

The cliffs are often described as sentries holding back the sea. I disagree. To me, they look like granite warriors preparing to march west to do battle. There is an ominous darkness to these buttressed cliffs that drop 700 feet into the Atlantic Ocean. They are angry, powerful and brutal in their beauty. After exiting the centre and reaching the platform of rock that drops straight down to the waves, I turned left. The walk up onto the headlands shows off the cliffs in their full glory. Within a hundred paces I joined the snail-like progression of tourists, all getting in the way of each other and not helped by one French child who was determined to slip through the railings, much to the horror of his parents.

171

I paused against the railings and looked south along the 8-kilometre stretch of cliffs. At the southernmost end, where some of these tourists may have been heading, is a rocky outcrop known as Hag's Head. I wasn't going that far. I looked down into the ocean and watched the swell transform from immense blue to blistering white. Thierry had talked about surfing along this coastline, but no surfer in their right mind would dare to ride these violent waves . . . a surfer in their wrong mind most definitely would. John McCarthy has made something of a career out of surfing these crashing rollers. He even made a TV advertisement promoting Allied Irish Bank . . . now there's a crash if ever there was one.

Playing Lahinch Golf Club was a big event. Having recently played Ballybunion, I was about to enter the Ballybunion versus Lahinch debate. It is a fiercely contested discussion, for these are two venerable links.

The small seaside resort of Lahinch borders Liscannor Bay, with its long and wide beach that proves a magnet for families in summer. But Lahinch draws animals of two different varieties far more frequently: surfers and golfers. It is usually easy to identify one from the other: clothes, hair, equipment and waistline are the obvious giveaways. In 2006, forty-four surfers managed to ride one small wave in the bay to set a new world record. As a golfer, that doesn't sound very impressive to me but, as a kook, what did I know?

I was on the tee by 7 a.m. the next morning, chatting to my playing partner Martin Barrett. Martin is a man of some importance up this way and he is well known, both for his golfing prowess and his contributions to Lahinch Golf Club. Today, he looks after the Overseas Membership, but he is a man who plays links golf beautifully and he has the added gravitas of being able to pull off the pork-pie hat. When you play scratch golf for much of your life, you can get away with most fashion hiccups.

It was a joyful round of golf. Having a personal tour guide, caddie and storyteller always adds something special, and Martin had lots of stories to tell. Irish golf was the main topic of conversation. Some fascinating background on Doonbeg opened my eyes on course development but there were also tales from America, as well as his descriptions of Pebble Beach, Spy Glass and Cypress Point. He drove off first on every hole and showed me the way, which was essential on a rhythmic course that lulls you into its embrace before ripping out your insides.

For many golfers, the experience of playing a course that has been left untouched since the original designer first walked the land is a big part of the occasion. Who else has played these hallowed fairways? What did the greatest golfers of their day score on this hole? Did they have to endure this wind? How many shanked their ball into the dunes 50 yards right of the target? And which lucky sod is going to find my brand new Titleist ProV1? Courses like Royal County Down (Old Tom Morris and Harry Vardon), Royal Portrush (Harry Colt) and Royal Belfast (also Harry Colt), among others, still reflect the original designer's mark and vision. It is a privilege and an honour to play these courses, and there is little doubt that the 5th hole at Lahinch, named 'The Dell', is one of the greatest examples of all. Created by Old Tom Morris in 1894, the hole remains true to its original design and is one of the most famous holes in Ireland. This is partly due to its history, but also because it is a par three that rarely reveals the flag as the green is tucked behind two dunes.

For all its brilliance, Lahinch has one other thing going

for it: a pair of goats. We passed them on the 14th – one tethered, one free to roam.

'They predict the weather,' Martin informed me.

'Uh-huh,' I responded.

Martin wasn't having any of my doubts. 'If they stay close to the clubhouse, the weather won't be good, but if they're out on the course, like here, then we're in for a fine day.'

'And which weather front staked the big goat?' I asked.

'Oh, well, that one wanders.'

Back in the 1960s, the clubhouse barometer broke, so the secretary pasted over it with a sign that read: See Goats. And it has been a part of the club's folklore ever since, to the point that a goat is at the heart of their club emblem.

I played the comparatively lightweight Lahinch Castle course in the afternoon, before returning to Ennis and the warm embrace of Mark and Christine. It meant missing out on the village of Lisdoonvarna and the spectacular limestone Burren, but my hosts' three children had by now assumed that I was some long-lost uncle coming to live with them, so I didn't want to disappoint. I helped with the cooking that night. It was a welcome change to be chopping rather than hacking.

From Ennis, I headed towards the Slieve Aughty Mountains to the north and the town of Gort. Here, in the empty and enormous Gort Golf Club car park, I managed to crash into the clubhouse. Not content with parking in any of the hundred spaces, I decided to reverse into a small space at the back of the building, failing to notice an overhang. Several crunches and much ranting later, I parked elsewhere, averted my eyes from the new crack and stomped onto the golf course.

Like the Loch Ness Monster gliding through Scotland's dark waters, the builder's bum has become an increasingly rare sight in Ireland. During the 1990s and 2000s, Eastern European Man, fit and svelte, had no appreciation for our nation's sartorial etiquette, and the builder's bum slipped quietly back into unsuspecting underpants. As I entered Gort Golf Club, I discovered that, like the grey squirrel, Eastern European Man seemed not to have crossed the mighty Shannon. I walked into the changing rooms to be greeted by a six-inch grin of hairy bum crack, courtesy of a workman on his hands and knees, fixing the floor.

'You doing all right there?' I asked, averting my eyes. 'Can I use the showers?'

'I dunno,' came the reply. 'Ask inside.'

I did. I couldn't. I left, wondering when I should cover up the crack. You know which one I mean.

Galway City, and its three golf courses, was my turning point for home. From then on the camper was always pointed east as I played Athenry, Cregmore Park and Ballinasloe. There was still time to abuse the hospitality of one more friend on this trip. Padraic and his family live on the outskirts of Ballygar. I hadn't seen him since university and I arrived just as his wife was going out (smart lady) leaving me with Padraic and the kids (smarter lady still). Padraic cooked, the kids entertained and we caught up.

I didn't meet up with friends all the time – far from it – but it made me appreciate the simple things, the important things. I spoke to my wife every day by phone, but it wasn't the same as being face-to-face, and spending time with Padraic, Mark and Christine made me homesick. Sure, the travelling and golf were a blast, but life did get boring sitting in the camper van. This was my last full trip in the Republic of Ireland, and another six weeks in Northern Ireland would see this quest wrapped up. In some ways I didn't want it to end; in others, I did.

The trip home passed through Portumna, Nenagh, Thurles and Carrick-on-Suir, and it was Portumna that stood out in so many ways.

Golfers always want to know where they'll find the hidden gems, and they'll find one at Portumna Golf Club on the northern shores of Lough Derg. The course is bordered by deep forest, but the holes run across the old Clanricarde Estate, with solitary oak and beech trees lending important anchors to the course design, and tiers of stone wrapped around them adding intrigue. There are many of these piles around the golf course, rising up to eight feet and all looking like three-layered wedding cakes.

'They were built when the Estate was still in existence,' Michael Ryan told me when I returned to the clubhouse. 'The ladies of the day used them to watch the horse races.'

Combined with the dozens of deer that wander the course, Portumna is as much an idyllic stroll as a round of golf.

In the changing rooms I heard English accents. Six guys in their mid-fifties were preparing to go out.

'Where else have you played?' I asked, after introductions had been made.

'This is our last round. We played here already, as well as Nenagh, East Clare and . . . lads, what was the other course we played?'

Somewhere forgettable as between them they couldn't remember its name.

'We're on a five-day package and you get to choose which course to play again on the last day. We all chose here.'

'What did you think of Nenagh?' I had yet to play the course.

'Nice enough. No big shakes and easy enough to score on. Fantastic showers.'

Four of the guys said their goodbyes and headed out of the changing rooms.

'Did you hear about the fox at East Clare?' I asked. There were only two guys left, but my question stopped them. I had enjoyed my round at East Clare immensely. Probably the most peaceful golf course I'd ever visited, but the story I'd been told by Mike in the pro shop added that extra bit of colour.

'No,' they said in unison.

I was surprised. Seeing as they were English, I thought Mike would have gleefully told them the tale. 'There used to be a fox that was fed by members,' I began. 'He was almost tame, to the point he figured out how to raid unattended golf bags. He regularly unzipped bags to steal Mars bars and bananas, but on this occasion there was no chocolate or fruit, so he stole the next best thing . . . a wallet containing £4,000 sterling.'

I had their interest now.

'The wallet belonged to the organiser of a group of English guys, and he was in charge of the money. The fox ran off, with four guys legging after it into the wild stuff, but the fox was gone. The guys played on and when they were coming down the 18th, which runs parallel to the hole where the wallet was stolen, they ventured into the rough again and found the wallet.'

The guys laughed but I wasn't convinced they believed me. Hell, I didn't believe me, but it's a good story.

I made it to Nenagh Golf Club, sitting happily on the rolling hillsides of County Tipperary. A young man was coming off the course and Rusty attracted his attention. It turned out that Tom was the son of Louis O'Connor, a formidable member at my home club of Greystones. He asked if I'd like some company for nine holes, which turned into a full round of eighteen. It was easy to see from his stance on the 1st tee that Tom liked to hit the ball. He muscled up to the ball like it had misbehaved and he was going to teach it a lesson. Even the waggle of the clubhead behind the ball delivered an ominous message and before he started his first swing I remember thinking, 'I wouldn't want to be that ball.'

He had a fast, balanced swing that sent the ball a mile down the middle of the fairway. The trouble was, when he mistimed it, the ball launched in a giant hook that threatened neighbouring counties and shipping lanes. An amazing 'swoosh' tore off the ball as it rose into the sky, curled away and got lost in the clouds. But when he hit it straight, no par four was safe.

I drove on to play the last few courses before heading home.

Ireland, for generations, fought for its conscience and soul. It endured pain and despair and it thrived on its triumphs. It made the Irish stronger as a nation, while our resilience in the face of adversity made us a much-loved people around the world. Then came the Celtic Tiger, and boy did that beast have us in a stranglehold, choking us in its greed-laden grip. We towed the line, of course, drawn on by its irresistible force as we were lured into wanting more . . . more money, more power, more houses, more everything. We got so greedy, careless and carried away on a false wave of prosperity that our heads were so far up our asses we couldn't see daylight.

Everywhere I drove I saw the signs and nowhere was this more obvious than in the villages across the land. What had once been a small and quaint little community of a few houses, now had an estate of twenty glorified cardboard boxes bolted on to one end. It stuck out like a yardarm, from which new owners could hang themselves in the depths of mortgage debt. This wasn't just choking the life out of the people, ripping away our values and community spirit, this was choking the life out of Ireland.

Attitudes changed, too. The world owed us, our employers owed us. If we weren't making money, getting pay rises, earning whopping bonuses and driving bigger cars, then someone was at fault. Not us – somebody else.

In one shape or another this is what appeared every day on the news. It's what the reporters told us because the only 'good' news is bad news. It made you think we were irredeemable, and yet for many Irish people and those who had come to work here from overseas, it was about living day to day and getting by. Not everyone had the opportunity to get rich quick; not everyone was infected.

The Irish define their country as it defines them. Drive through our towns and watch the everyday life that consumes each one of us. Schoolchildren sitting on walls, laughing, chasing, dancing. Harassed mothers pushing prams with one hand, talking into mobile phones with the other. Joggers and cyclists wearing Lycra, headphones and carrying bottled water. Dogs walking, couples talking, teenagers fawning over each other. It could be any country in the world. Drive through an Irish village and you'll see a pub or three, perhaps one with a grocery store out back, a post office and not a lot else. Our culture thrives on the pub environment. Even now, with the smoking ban and the random breath-testing and the hundreds of pubs closing every year, there is still a pub and a pint at the heart of most communities.

So, drive through that village, avoid the cardboard buildings and look for the pubs. Look for the old man sitting outside, waiting, wearing his flat cap and appreciate the beauty of the cliché. And if you stop and talk to him be prepared for an ear bending. If there's one thing the Irish like more than a sociable pint, it's a sociable pint berating the politics of Ireland. Lord knows, we have plenty to complain about now.

I passed through so many of these villages that they merged into a blur. A sense of déjà vu would hit me and only the different patterns of life broke the spell.

I was heading out of Carrick-on-Suir, still in County Tipperary, driving up a hill that had Rusty wheezing. An old car rattled along in front of me, its exhaust making up for the country's no smoking ban. As we approached a sharp bend the car slowed, slowed some more and then stopped in the middle of the road. No indication, nothing. The driver got out, leaving the door open, and wandered across the road towards the corner shop. And then he turned to me and waved. He was an old fella, wearing a ratty tweed jacket, mucky black trousers and wellington boots. A farmer if ever there was one.

There was no way I was going to overtake on a blind corner – not in a vehicle that goes from nought to sixty in an hour and a half – so I grabbed my map and tried to figure out where I'd find Carrick-on-Suir Golf Club. I was having no joy and there was no sign of the farmer, so I switched off the engine, clambered out of the camper and went to join him. The farmer's car was still running

The girl in the shop looked over my shoulder as I entered, wondering no doubt what all the hooting was about. The farmer was at the counter and he turned to me as I approached, a smile creasing his face.

'Good lad,' he said gruffly, the wrinkles in his face squeezing together. 'It's a slow day.'

Evidently.

He took his change and headed off while the girl in the shop gave me directions. As I walked back across the road, the hooting intensified. I looked at the five cars behind the camper van, I smiled and waved like the farmer had, but all I got in return were shouted insults I pretended not to hear.

As I switched on the engine, the farmer finally pulled away and, in a slow funeral-like procession, we headed up the steep and windy R676 doing no more than 30 km/h – he because it was a 'slow day', and me because I couldn't go any faster on such a hill.

Yes indeed, there were places that the Celtic Tiger hadn't reached and one of those places was inside the car in front of me.

Bottoms Up

'Is my friend in the bunker or is the bastard on the green?'

DAVID FEHERTY

When I was growing up, I always saw the Troubles in Northern Ireland as being a long way away, not affecting my small, everyday life . . . at least not until bomb warnings in Dublin closed down the street where my girlfriend worked. And when I went for interviews at Queen's University in Belfast in 1985, and came face-to-face with two enormous policemen carrying rifles, I acquired a far greater respect for the difficulties affecting the people across the Border.

By the 2000s, I was under the impression that much had been improved. Guns handed in, wall murals painted over, sentry posts and barbed wire compounds dismantled. The Good Friday Agreement had done so much for our two countries, and people north and south held their heads high.

But that didn't mean everything was trouble-free.

I was making calls to arrange tee times and I contacted

Clandeboye Golf Club in Conlig, County Down. There was no issue with my visit . . . to start with.

'When do you want to play?' the woman asked me.

'The twelfth.'

'The twelfth . . . of July?' There was a lengthy pause. 'I don't think that's going to work. That's the start of marching season. It wouldn't be . . .' (there was a long pause at the other end of the phone as she searched for the right word) 'prudent to park here with a Republic of Ireland number plate.'

As it turned out, I didn't have to worry about 12 July. Rusty had other plans, tearing the timing belt before I had moved from beside the house.

Talking to, swearing at and assaulting inanimate objects is a pointless exercise, if an extremely satisfying one. I watched in a cold rage as Morgan carted the camper van away on his tow truck, telling me it would be ready in a week. I picked up the phone and rescheduled all my visits.

The following week, as promised, Morgan called from the garage. Everything was fixed.

I arrived to see Rusty being driven out for a final test run. On its return, I climbed in, started it up and smiled as the engine roared into life. I put it into reverse. It didn't go. I tried first, second, third and fourth with no joy at all. No, it couldn't be. There was no way this was happening. From happiness to despair in the blink of an eye. In my fury, I tried fifth and sixth gears, which is saying something for a camper van with only four, but Rusty was unmoved. The gear stick simply wouldn't budge.

Rusty's dislike for me wasn't instant. No, like any great relationship we had to work at it, the antagonism developing slowly over time. I tried to establish a rapport, to use reason and logic, but Rusty would shrug and pout and refuse to comply. I wanted to drive to the next course; Rusty felt inclined to stay put. I wanted to cook; Rusty preferred a night in the clubhouse bar. I wanted to stay dry . . .

And now I was squeezed into the corner of a garage lot with, literally, no place to turn. It was at that moment that we came to a mutual understanding: Rusty could do whatever he damn well pleased and I had to live with that.

Morgan wandered over to see what all the noise was about. Grinding the gears can sound like a death rattle after all. When I mentioned Rusty's reluctance to move, Morgan scratched his head, scratched his chin and then stuck a finger in his ear. None of these tactics proved successful, so he told me he'd need the camper van for another week.

As it turned out, in those few moments between test drive and me reclaiming the driver's seat, the cable clutch had snapped.

More phone calls followed as the goodwill shown to me by the North's golf clubs began to evaporate.

When I finally set off a week later, it appeared, ironically, that the golfing gods had been kind to me. During that week the North had endured torrential rain that caused widespread flooding, burst riverbanks and landslides. Two bridges collapsed and dozens of major roads were closed, including part of the M1 motorway.

I played my way steadily north, driving through north Dublin and into that thin wedge of County Meath that boasts 10 kilometres of coastline. Golf courses rattled by: Hollywood Lakes, Balbriggan, Skerries and Bellewstown. At Laytown & Bettystown, County Meath's only links course, things got a bit ugly when the clubhouse alarm went off at 3 a.m. The committee member who turned up discovered me walking around and concluded I was responsible. I couldn't blame him under the circumstances, and we had a ding-dong as I explained who I was and tried to stop him calling the gardaí. Then it was into County Louth to play Baltray, Seapoint, Ballymascanlon and Dundalk.

I finally crossed the Border on my way to Cloverhill Golf Club in Mullaghbawn.

I struggled to find my way along the winding roads, not far from the notorious Crossmaglen. This was a hotbed for the IRA during The Troubles and the site of dozens of murders. The rural roads eventually directed me to the club. Surrounded by the volcanic Ring of Gullion, the scenery is a curve of green and rolling hills.

The cosy clubhouse was home to a barman and a table of four lads. I introduced myself and was promptly passed a pint.

The barman, Colin, turned out to be the club's manager, greenkeeper and pretty much everything else.

We chatted and he introduced me to the other four residents, and that's how I met Tony, the resident Pro. He looked a bit portly to my eye, which is rich coming from me. The golf shirt was stretched around his middle, which hung rather precariously over the top of his trousers. He bought me a pint and asked a few polite questions about my travels. He paused and then started to ask a question that had clearly been forming for some time.

'So how much will you make from this book? You'll make thousands, right?'

I thought of the cost of the camper van, the diesel, the breakdowns, the food and drink (free pints aside), my working income sacrificed . . . and I balanced this against my small book advance.

'Not exactly,' I offered. 'This is more for the love of golf, not the love of money.'

Tony looked surprised. 'But you're getting free green fees?' He was forming a plan. 'You see, I'm thinking of doing something similar myself.'

'Well,' I said, 'I imagine that as a Pro all the clubs will happily welcome you.'

He looked dubious as his companions roared laughing.

I turned to Colin who had a broad smile on his face. I realised I was being played. It turned out that Tony played off 19, but had taken to calling himself 'Tony the Pro' following forty-four points in the Captain's Prize.

As Tony and his pals left, Colin's mother dropped by to ask if I'd like some food. Never mind the free pints, I now had someone offering to fix my dinner. After my initial embarrassment, and her insistence, she headed back home to get to work.

I sat with Colin, discussing the club. He was a young lad, no more than twenty-five, and he had taken on the enterprise to keep it going. We discussed his work. He had no illusions of grandeur but was putting his heart and soul into the place.

At 6 a.m. the next morning someone tapped on the door three times. I wondered fleetingly if Colin's mum had arrived with a cooked breakfast, or maybe Tony had decided to join me. I was wrong on both counts.

As the door opened outwards, I was greeted by a cacophony of disgruntled quacking.

'What the . . .?'

Three ducks milled around in a flurry, all wings and aggravation, while a fourth stared at me indignantly. I'd knocked him off the step, from where he had been trying to say good morning. I'd seen them the day before and they'd seemed friendly. Now, not so much.

The golf club is never going to draw much in the way of

international visitors, but holes 8 to 12 are worth the modest green fee alone. They use a wild and rocky hillside, and a small lake that is home to the aforementioned ducks. An errant tee shot on the 9th plunged into the water and the ducks got mad. This was not proving a happy relationship.

Neither was the relationship with my golf shoes. They were so abused by that point that I assumed any waterproofing abilities had long gone. I had several pairs. They were divided into good shoes, bad shoes and back-up shoes. Ten rounds a week meant that I wore all of them, leaving the back-up shoes till last and praying it didn't rain. The difference between the categories was dictated by how much the leather was cracked and split. Even so, the good €120 shoes I was wearing at Cloverhill had another surprise in store. The sole and the upper decided to part company somewhere along the 12th fairway. Each step was accompanied by a slapping sound as the sole started flapping about like a half dead trout and smelling twice as bad.

Fortunately, my golf bag was also falling apart so I had a role of tape to hand. I wrapped it around my shoe a few times to hold it together and completed my round with one soaking wet foot. In the clubhouse I tossed the shoes in the bin. I was so fed up that two other pairs from the camper van followed – my apologies to Cloverhill if you had to call in the fumigators. That left me with exactly one new pair of Footjoys . . . and sixty rounds of golf to go.

Shoes weren't the only equipment to be binned: one trolley and one golf bag had already gone to the grave, the bag spilling a neglected collection of Irish coins that had last seen the light of day a decade before.

When I stepped into the clubhouse, I told Colin about my duck encounters.

He laughed. 'The ducks wander into the clubhouse and the changing rooms from time to time. Our members have often stepped into the shower to be greeted by the entire family.'

They were probably hiding from golfers on the 9th tee.

I returned to the southern side of the border in County Monaghan. Concra Wood was a brand new course still under construction but Karen, their marketing girl, had been more than happy to accommodate me.

There was one problem with the course being under construction, and that problem was mud.

I was 50 yards up the steep driveway when I hit it. The rains of recent weeks had churned this track into a marsh with deep ruts where vehicles had carved their way up the hillside. Singularly unprepared for the terrain, the camper van slipped and slid from side to side, the little wheels spinning like billy-o as they fought for traction.

'Come on,' I roared idiotically as I begged and pleaded for the van to keep going. My foot pressed further down on the accelerator until it threatened to break through the floor. The rear end started to drift away towards an ominously deep and mud-filled hollow. I could see the local paper's next headline: Submerged camper van towed from mud bath. Driver charged with stupidity.

With some skilful manoeuvring and a lot of cursing I made it to the construction site halfway up. I was sweating hard as I put on some golf shoes and stumbled out to the bemusement of two workers who had watched my progress.

'You're that golfer bloke, aren't ye?' said the taller of the two. 'Karen said she'd meet you at the bottom of the hill.' They turned away laughing. 'She said not to try driving up through the mud.'

I looked around for something to throw at them and

that's when I saw the side of the camper van. Streaks of mud reaching eight feet high were sprayed from front to back in an elegant arc. The other side was worse.

'You must be Kevin,' came the voice. 'I see you made it up the hill.'

'Yes,' I replied, turning to face Karen. 'No problems at all,' I said, nonchalantly trying to block the twelve-foot-wide swathe of mud behind me.

I could see Karen's eyes drift to the camper van and the evidence of my epic struggle.

'Hmm,' she responded.

We shook hands and I noted Karen's elegant dress, finished off with a pair of wellington boots. I looked down at my own shoes and realised I might be in trouble.

'Shall we go?'

Her four-wheel drive had once been blue, but was now a solid shade of mud. I climbed in and Karen gunned the engine. She looked small behind the wheel as we drove off and her blonde hair contrasted with the dark patch on the roof above her head. I frowned and started to look at the roof above my own head.

'I wouldn't . . .' she started to say, but it was too late. A pothole had sent us both skywards and while the top of her head collided with the roof, it was my upturned face that took the brunt of the impact.

'I'm so sorry,' she started to say as we went airborne again. She eased off the accelerator and I had time to readjust my nose. She was trying hard not to laugh and I could feel that sense of stupidity returning . . . although it had never really gone away.

Karen was the marketing and sales manager for the club. She was young, smart and very enthusiastic, but her marketing spiel faded into the background as we reached the crest of the hill and the stunning vista burst open before us. Concra Wood sits above Lake Muckno, fingers of land edging into the water, grasping the lake in its embrace. Islands with trees marching down to the shore are splashed about like confetti and all around are views stretching over the rolling drumlins.

'Impressive, isn't it!' a voice said beside me.

It brought me back down to earth and, as Karen drove me around the course, along the muddy, potholed tracks that were steadily giving me a screaming headache, I realised that Concra Wood would be every bit as beautiful as its setting.

Golf has the universal advantage of being open to people of all ages. It used to be that Juniors were of the seen-and-not-heard variety, but today they are embraced as the future of the game. Being allowed to dictate TV policy in the clubhouse bar, however, is another matter entirely.

Heading back cross the Border, thereby switching road names and numbers once again, I walked into the Portadown Golf Club bar to be greeted by SpongeBob Squarepants. Not exactly what I was expecting. In clubhouses, TV equals Sky News or Sky Sports. Here the programming was designed to appease an audience of two avid young girls, while other youngsters raced about between the tables. Peals of laughter were tempered by words of caution from parents on different tables, but there was a great buzz to the place and a sense of joy. Mostly.

One child was not participating, despite his mother's urging. He sat with his arms folded and a deep frown of frustration descending between his eyes.

'Go on,' the mother said, 'go and play with the others.'

'No,' came the churlish reply.

'Why not?'

'They're too young.'

The mother was bemused. 'But they're the same age as you.'

The son's face scrunched into a mask of incredulity. 'They are not, Mummy,' he said with a contempt a politician would have been proud of. 'They're four, and I'm four and three quarters.'

He rolled his eyes and returned to his fizzy orange, ending what he deemed to be a pointless conversation.

The mother looked across at me and shrugged.

From Portadown I headed northeast on the busy A3, playing courses in Lurgan, Silverwood, Edenmore and Down Royal.

A road sign announced 'Maze' and, as I took the turning, it was impossible not to think immediately of The Maze prison, something everyone my age in Ireland knows about. Known for its H-shaped buildings, so distinctive from the air, it housed paramilitary prisoners for over thirty years during The Troubles. It was closed in 2000, but for the three decades it was open it garnered worldwide attention on more than one occasion. Top of the list are the hunger strikes of 1980 and 1981. The latter claimed the lives of ten men, most famously Bobby Sands who died on the sixty-sixth day of his hunger strike. During this period he was voted a Member of Parliament, and, for his funeral, some 100,000 people lined the streets.

Did it achieve anything? That depends on your point of view. It raised the profile of the Republican movement, the poor conditions in which H-Block prisoners were held and, ultimately, the political aspirations of Sinn Féin. But it cost ten men their lives and, whatever the cause, that was too high a price to pay.

Most of The Maze had been demolished by the time I

drove past it. Behind a single line of houses, on the aptly named Gravehill Road, I could see no sign of the structures that had appeared endlessly on the television in my teenage years.

On the opposite side of the road, white railings weaved in and out of view, revealing a racetrack and, beyond, the unmistakeable shape of golf holes. I had no idea what to expect of Down Royal Golf Club, but the location inside a racetrack was my first surprise. It's not that uncommon a feature in Ireland, with Leopardstown, Navan and Gowran Park all requiring similar ventures inside the rails, but here there were horses and jockeys out on the track and, from a distance, it looked like they were thundering over the golf course itself.

'Any idea where I'll find Billy?' I asked the man near the door, shortly after parking.

He glanced up and then behind him as a crash resounded from somewhere inside. 'Now what's she up to?' he sighed.

I followed him to a small glass-walled cubicle that fronted as an office. Inside, on the floor, was a little girl of six or seven attempting to send faxes. Fingers poked liberally at the numbers and when she hit the right one a sheet of paper would spool out.

'Papa,' she'd yelp with glee.

As he bent to pick her up and rescue the fax machine he asked which Billy I was looking for.

'Billy McCaffin.'

'Ahh,' he said, 'you want Billy One. I'm Billy Two. Billy One's on holiday.'

There can't be many clubs where the only two full-time members of staff are called Billy. They manage the clubhouse and are the course's greenkeepers, too, and as Billy shooed me out to the 1st tee before a group arrived, I was reminded of Colin at Cloverhill and all the work he did. Greenkeepers are the most under-appreciated people on the golf course . . . by golfers at least.

Down Royal has soft turf that dispels water almost as soon as it lands. It's a blessing and it creates a surface that has a certain spring to it. And that makes it ripe for gorse, or furze as the Americans call it. Either way, it's prickly stuff and when I got back to the camper, I dropped my trousers and picked gorse thorns from places no thorn should ever be allowed to go. Sometimes, where a ball ventures there is no need to follow.

Afterwards, in the clubhouse, Billy was serving behind the bar. He introduced me to Ian, Michael and Tommo at a nearby table. A chair was pushed backwards and three enquiring faces waited for my thoughts.

'That's a lot of gorse out there.'

The three boys nodded slowly at my words of wisdom. Actually, they stared at me like I was an idiot.

Billy thumped a pint down on the table. 'On the house,' he said to me, before glaring at the others. 'Leave it alone, lads. I warned ye.'

'Have you played at Spa yet?' Tommo wanted to know as Billy moved away.

'A very enjoyable parkland,' I replied of the club in County Down.

'It is, it is. I imagine you're after a few good stories for your book.' When I nodded he continued. 'I have one for you, and I know it's true because I know the guys who were playing.

'Back when Spa was a nine-hole course, they were on the 3rd hole. One of the boys, John, tees up and smashes his drive into the huge tree on the left of the tee. The ball never reappears, so he reloads. But he hits his second shot into the same tree, never to be seen again.'

I sat back and smiled. Judging by the cadences, Tommo had reeled this one off a good few times.

'So he reloads again and he hits the same tree. There's no sign of the ball so John, fuming like a truck, stomps off back to the clubhouse. That night, at about 2 a.m., neighbours near the club call the police because of noisy activity on the golf course. When the police arrive they discover John, with a chainsaw, cutting down the offending tree.'

He leaned back, watching my reaction. 'Gospel truth,' he proclaimed.

We've all had our bad days, our secret rages, our black clouds, but holding a grudge against an inanimate object for over twelve hours is taking things a bit far. I imagined John sitting in the dark slowly stroking his chainsaw, laughing malevolently . . . and I worried for his health.

The road to Belfast, the A3, had taken me through Lurgan and on to Lisburn, and then on to Dunmurry, via the A512. I played golf with the walkers, the talkers, the hitters and the bullshitters. I played with the silent ones, the angry ones, the perfectionists and the over-analysis-nothing's-quite-as-it-should-be ones. Dave was one of the last types. He was my sort of age, with tight curly hair and an expression that suggested life was one disappointment after another. On Lisburn's 1st tee, even as the ball left the clubface, he was critiquing the shot: 'No, no, that's going left. I didn't . . .' he paused as he held the pose of his follow through, '. . . I didn't get the clubhead through the ball, too lazy with my hips.' He took a couple of swings to illustrate what he should have done. 'Like that,' he muttered as he stepped away from the tee.

The same happened on the second and third shots, and

the three putts. It turned into one of those rounds where there was a lot of talk and very little conversation.

Belfast City was now fixed on the horizon, its scattering of tall buildings rising above the trees. On its outskirts, I was to find two of the most highly-regarded parkland courses in Northern Ireland: Malone and Belvoir Park. I had been warned about Malone, for their sniffy attitude and their treatment of visitors. What I hadn't been told was that it was a hotbed for the wealthy Belfastistas. My arrival in a 1989 camper van raised a few eyebrows on a Saturday morning. One particular member watched in horror, hands clasped to his face, as I reversed into a small space beside his Jag. It was OK though as I missed his car entirely and only scraped the Porsche on the other side. Seriously, his reaction implied that even the draft created by Rusty was likely to damage his precious car. Or maybe he'd just never seen a camper van before.

'Morning to you,' I chirped breezily as I walked past. His lips flapped but no sound escaped.

I heard a lot more of the club's history from Michael, who found me in the bar and enquired if I was the man writing the book. He asked if he could join me and I spent the next two hours in some very friendly company. A wizened old soul, Michael had silver hair and dark, bushy eyebrows that hung down like windscreen wipers. He had an expressive face and his eyebrows twitched constantly, as if a torrential downpour was interfering with his line of sight.

I laid my cards on the table. 'I heard that a golf writer from England came to play here a while back and wrote a scathing review of the treatment he received.'

Michael pursed his lips with displeasure. 'Yes, we weren't very happy about that.' He shifted in his chair and leaned forward, lowering his voice, 'But these things happen. People have bad days. Malone is . . .' he searched for the words. 'Malone is an old institution with grand old ways. Strict dress codes, the order of things, visitors should be seen but not heard . . . you know what I'm getting at?'

I did, but it didn't detract one bit from the pleasure of playing one of Ireland's sweetest parklands.

Driving from one course to the next I got lost only once or twice . . . well, a few times . . . OK, a lot. Did I stop and ask for directions? I would rather stick needles in my eyes.

I got lost so often that it was an expected part of the day and I factored this into the journey-time. Too many times I drove along country lanes that clearly had never considered that someone in a camper van might need to turn around. Trying to find Mannan Castle in County Monaghan, I drove endlessly up a track with grass running down the middle, looking for somewhere I could turn. I ended up in a farmyard. In the field next to me, a farmer and his dog were corralling sheep. The farmer stopped; the dog stopped; even the sheep stopped to see what had interrupted their daily routine. As I noisily cranked a gear and cursed in my efforts to make a quick getaway, the dog summed up my performance with a patronising tilt of its head.

The ability to stop and ask a stranger for directions eludes us. We'd rather drive until the diesel runs out so we can shake our heads and sigh 'well, we almost made it' than look for help. On the way from Malone to Belvoir Park, following the A55, I'd finally passed that point. I pulled over, parked and started banging my head against the steering wheel.

'Can I help?' asked the voice of a kindly man passing by. 'You look lost.'

'Do you know how I get to Belvoir Park?' I asked, once the stars had cleared.

'It's easy,' said the man, thereby dooming me to further disaster before he'd even started.

He was wrapped in a long jacket that flapped around him as he raised an arm and pointed in the direction I was going. 'Go down here about a mile, until you get to the petrol station. Turn left. Then blah until the blah, and follow that road for blah. At the lights b-b-b-b-blah. Once you reach the blah it's right there. You can't miss it.' Then he turned to face me. 'You got that or do you want me to go through it again?'

'Nope, that's perfect,' I said. 'Couldn't be easier. Thanks very much.' I drove on, pulled into the petrol station and opened the map. When that didn't work, I asked somebody else.

I did find Belvoir Park . . . eventually. Perhaps it was ironic that after getting lost so many times the club wasn't expecting me until the following day.

At least my next stop proved much easier to find. Shandon Park is another 'old' club, dating back to 1926, and inside I sat behind a group of golden oldies who may well have been the club's most elderly members. Their voices were slightly raised as photographs of great-grandkids were passed around and the correct oohs and aahs greeted the viewing of each new picture. The elder statesman, a man small and bent with glasses perched on the end of his nose, then started recounting a war story . . . and I don't mean his triple bogey on the 15th. I only caught snippets, but I heard reference to approaching German tanks, scalding hot metal and the Libyan stronghold of Tobruk, which was an important strategic port during the Second World War. He talked about the time a Spitfire was grounded and how he and his comrades repaired it, ready for action again. I'm sorry I didn't hear more, and I'm sorrier still that I didn't get out of my seat and go over and introduce myself. Soon there will be no veterans left, and the memories that these remarkable men and women carry around with them will be consigned to history, accessible only through books and the Internet. How much better would it have been to hear it from the horse's mouth and let this man know that there are still so many of us out there who appreciate the sacrifices he made and the battles he waged 'in our name'. We will never understand the conditions of war that he endured and that are, today, so trivialised through an X-Box or Playstation.

'Are you the gobshite who liked Scrabo?' Ricky asked me in the bluntest of terms when I introduced myself in Knock's pro shop. Considering the club is no more than a 5 iron from the entrance to Stormont, home to the Northern Assembly, I would have preferred something more politically correct. And after finding my way to Knock without getting lost once, I was hoping for praise, not abuse.

Scrabo was a course I had already played and was soon to revisit. I guess when you stick your neck out and express an opinion, as I had done in a *Belfast Telegraph* article, you need skin thick enough to take the criticism. I gave the Pro a smile. 'What can I say, I love the place. You're not a fan, I take it?'

He shook his head. 'Jesus wept.'

I wasn't aware that Jesus had played enough courses to form an opinion.

Knock is a grand course, but I'd play Scrabo ahead of it . . . not that I said that to the Pro.

I was heading east, visiting Carnalea, Rockmount, Bangor, Royal Belfast, Blackwood and Clandeboye, all along the A2 main road on the southern side of Belfast Lough. I rarely saw the water, but through the endless tapestry of housing estates and villages, views of the Belfast hills flickered in and out of view.

Immediately after Knock, however, came Holywood Golf Club, a course that few outside Holywood had ever heard of until a certain Rory McIlroy came along. The course rises up a hillside, offering views over Belfast. The gantry cranes (Samson and Goliath) of the Harland & Wolff shipyard drew my eye as they rose like yellow croquet hoops above the skyline. Inside the clubhouse, what drew my eye was the ever-growing Rory McIlroy Wall of Fame.

While I was digesting his course records at places like Royal Portrush (61 at age sixteen), the boy wonder himself was sitting in the members' bar only a few feet away. I only found out after he'd left. At least I got to play the course he grew up on and the one so popular with nuns. I have to confess that I'd never seen a nun in full swing, nor any other type of swing for that matter. I'd always assumed that the habit would be a liability, causing all kinds of discomfort on the take-away. And then there's the headgear. Holywood, though, had embraced them and gave them right of way as was evident from the sign behind the 5th green:

> Golfers
> Beware of Traffic When Crossing
> Nuns Walk to Play 6th Hole

I read it twice to appreciate the gravity of the statement. I glanced around, half expecting a line of nuns to make an appearance with golf bags slung across their backs. Somehow, nuns pulling trolleys felt wrong. I also wondered how many nuns it took for them to be regarded as 'traffic', or was 'traffic' the collective noun for nuns?

When I arrived on the 6th tee I was somewhat disappointed to find the hole nun-less. I waited patiently until I glanced at the scorecard and discovered the hole is called Nuns Walk, which is the name of the lane up to the club. Too bad: I could have told them some cracking jokes about priests playing golf.

There have been a number of signs at golf courses that cause confusion – none more so than Royal County Down's instruction to women: 'Women may wear trousers on the golf course but must remove them before entering the clubhouse.'

After my round, I hung about like a lost puppy in the vain hope that Rory might return. Some chance. I packed up and made my way towards Clandeboye to the east, outside Conlig, a small village where Eddie Irvine was raised.

The words of the girl from Clandeboye Golf Club were ringing in my ears as I turned into the club car park later that afternoon.

'It wouldn't be sensible to park here with a Republic of Ireland number plate,' she'd said.

When a car pulled up the following morning and a man got out, throwing me a cheery wave and a 'good morning Kevin', I felt myself relax for the first time in many hours. Shane Derby worked for Open Fairways, and had the glorious title of Director of Golf Affairs.

The sun was burning through the morning mist as we stood on the 1st tee for the day's competition. It made a mockery of the previous night's rain as views over Bangor and out to Belfast Lough opened up before us.

The clubhouse and two courses at Clandeboye will certainly impress visitors but, at a cool £1.5 million, the building is almost too big. With so many doors to choose from, Shane walked into a cleaning cupboard on one occasion when we were looking for the bar (and was thereafter nicknamed

George W.), and into the buggy storeroom when he was looking for the pro shop. It's that kind of a maze.

I tried to tempt Shane to join me at Scrabo Golf Club, a fifteen-minute drive to the south, but he had a job to do, even if it was to talk golf all day. A shame really as my second visit to Scrabo was blessed by sunshine. I drove up Scrabo Hill towards the tower that bears the hill's name. Built as a memorial to Charles Stewart, the third Marquess of Londonderry, in 1857, it dominates the skyline and is visible from almost everywhere on the golf course.

Scrabo is an adventure like no other. It can be brutally difficult but both the challenges and the surroundings are astounding. As I played over the bumpy fairways it was like being reunited with a long-lost friend. Scrabo Tower sits above the 1st green and it looks as inaccessible as some of the golf holes on this course. That said, I'd rather try and climb the tower's vertical walls than go looking for a ball in Scrabo's gorse. Perhaps it has been genetically modified, because this is the nastiest, sharpest stuff I have ever encountered – nastier even than Down Royal. I played with Maeve and Nick, a charming couple from Borris, County Carlow, and after only a couple of holes any ball that went into the gorse was left there. Even so, Scrabo was, and remains, one of the highlights of my travels.

My Northern Ireland journey was going better than I had hoped. I had not yet seen much of Northern Ireland's acclaimed beauty – Scrabo aside – but the people, whether at golf clubs, laundrettes or offering directions, were warm and generous . . . until I got to Kirkistown Castle.

The golf course is the most easterly course in Ireland, situated on the Ards Peninsula. As I drove from the north, still on the A2, I looked east, across the Irish Sea, to the Isle of Man and Scotland's Rhins of Galloway. As at Ceann Sibéal, I was looking for flags by the water only to find the links hidden away on the other side of the road. The car park revealed nothing of a little links that packs punch, which was what I had in mind for two particular golfers I was about to encounter.

I arrived at the club at 6.30 a.m., and was standing on the 1st tee using my driver to stretch. I had my golf ball on the tee and I was thinking of firing away, when out of the mist two golfers appeared. I thought I would have company for my round. I was wrong.

They stepped around my bag and walked onto the tee with drivers in hand. Both were in their fifties. One was tall and bulky with a flat cap pulled low; the other was shorter and skinnier, his nose a testament to a life of heavy drinking.

'Good morning,' I said, generously assuming they hadn't seen me in the mist, although they had passed close enough for me to kick.

One of them grunted at me but that was as eloquent as it got.

He bent down, teed up, and without another sound or look he hit his tee shot.

The second man followed suit. At that point I still held on to the vague hope that I would be invited to tee up next, but they walked off the tee and down the fairway. I was dumbfounded. There was no one within an ass's roar of where we were and these two had not only blanked me, they had cut in as if I didn't exist. Never in all my years have I encountered such ignorance on a golf course.

They hadn't hit very far and I could see them searching for one of their balls. I waited, and waited some more. They weren't inclined to acknowledge me so I strode up to my ball and drove over their heads. I was raging and I had reached such a level of fury that I would have taken a club to them if they'd said a word.

During my travels I had bad encounters at only a few golf clubs. At one club I was treated like a leper by the barman one night and then like a burglar by the same man the following day. At another, the general manager turned his back on me and walked away as I was talking to him. There is no place for such attitudes in golf.

After my round at Kirkistown Castle, I was still seething as I took a seat in the old clubhouse. Fortunately, a very charming woman came and took my breakfast order.

She winced at the look on my face. 'Bad round, sugar? We'll soon put a smile on your face.'

And she did. I ordered the works: the full Northern Irish breakfast.

For the uninitiated, the 'full' Irish, Northern Irish, English, Scottish and Welsh breakfasts are very much alike. You will receive sausages, bacon, egg, mushrooms and tomatoes. This is the healthy fried foundation to which each country then adds its own signature. In Ireland you'll receive black and white pudding. In Wales, it's cockles and laverbread, while Scotland throws in potato scones, oatcake and haggis. Here the speciality is farl, a type of soda bread that is split in half and then – you guessed it – fried.

'Could you leave off the tomatoes and mushrooms?' I asked. They are two vegetables I detest, no matter how deep-fried they are.

'Of course.' She gave me a wink. 'I'm sure we can give you something else.'

'Something else' it transpired was two extra sausages, rashers, a second egg and a gallon of beans oozing over the plate's edge in a last ditch attempt to escape. When she put the plate down, the food sat there like a heart attack waiting to happen.

'Enjoy,' she said with another wink and a smile that suggested she'd made sure my request had been over-indulged.

I'd ordered breakfast, not my dinner requirements for a week. I managed to eat a third of it. The remainder – but not the beans – was wrapped in a napkin and slipped into my pocket for later consumption. Anything was better than reheated pasta.

I continued down the peninsula to the southern tip and a stretch of water separating Portaferry and Strangford, where a ferry chugs merrily back and forth at the entrance to Strangford Lough, known as The Narrows. There are only partial views of Ireland's largest sea inlet, studded with islands, but merely to be standing at the boat's railing with the smell of the sea and the warmth of the sun on my back was a blissful time-out. I smiled as I spotted Scrabo Tower, no more than a matchstick in the distance.

Ahead of me lay one of the world's greatest courses – Royal County Down – but there was one unforgettable experience to come before I reached its hallowed turf.

When I stepped into the pro shop at Ardglass Golf Club I was surrounded by Americans buying enough Ardglass-branded merchandise to fill a camper van. That was both a good and a bad sign: good because it meant the course must be a decent track; bad because if I ended up playing behind them I'd be out there for six hours. After Tralee, it was not something I wished to repeat. Not even the Americans would dispute that their pace of golf is of the glacial variety, especially on vacation.

'What do you play off?' the man behind the counter asked when I checked in.

'Seven,' I told him.

He nodded thoughtfully. 'I'll see if I can find someone to join you, but I'll be sure to get you out before these guys. Grab some lunch and come back in forty minutes.'

The clubhouse at Ardglass is one of the most spectacular you'll find anywhere. It merges with the fifteenth-century Ardglass Castle and sits on the Irish Sea. Waves crash against rocks only a few metres away and one look at the 1st tee box will tell you that you could get soaked on a windy day.

The group of Americans, sixteen-strong, was already in the bar. One guy was clearly in charge, giving instructions and tee-time allocations. Once he'd finished, I tapped him on the shoulder. I had questions and I didn't beat around the bush.

'Where are you playing on this trip?'

American golfers come in two guises: the relaxed, do-it-yourself golfer who will take his or her time playing the courses that matter to them – like Roy and Stella in Killarney; and the kamikaze golfer who is determined to drive all night, play golf all day, drink Guinness and whiskey and see Ireland from the inside of a bus. Maybe it's hypocritical, given my own journey, but to these guys I want to say 'slow down, take your time'. See, experience and enjoy the beauty and charms of our small island.

David O'Rourke of O'Rourke's Irish Golf Crusade was escorting a tour of the kamikaze variety. They were in Ireland for seven days and playing seven courses that stretched from Royal Portrush to Old Head of Kinsale.

He was telling me about how he chose the courses and how his small Vermont tour operation worked. I liked the personal touches and he loved golfing in Ireland.

'Ever hear of Scrabo Golf Club?' I was prepared to bet that he hadn't.

He shook his head. 'Should I?' The corner of his mouth twitched as if he could taste a juicy bit of inside information.

I reported my experiences to David, expecting him politely to turn his nose up at the prospect, but it was quite the opposite. He was intrigued and asked for more details, promising to visit it on a forthcoming trip.

Back in the pro shop I asked the man if he'd found anyone willing to play with me. He had.

'Who?' I asked.

'Me,' Philip replied. 'Give me a sec and I'll get someone to cover the shop.'

My heart sank as he disappeared out the back. Philip Farrell was the club Pro and I felt distinctly uncomfortable at the prospect of playing with someone that good.

He shouted back through the doorway. 'Oh, and I only play from the back sticks.'

I headed to the 1st tee, looking at the scorecard. The tips added another 450 metres. I took a breath, preparing myself for a long day.

David walked over and handed me his company DVD. 'You're out right ahead of us. Enjoy.'

I stood on the back tee, a row of cannons poking me in the backside, and glanced across at the Americans who were all watching with curiosity as Philip arrived. We shook hands – I hoped he didn't feel the tremble – and he gestured for me to play away.

Ardglass has one of the best opening stretches of golf holes anywhere, and I quickly lost my nervousness as I got stuck into the golf. Philip was a gent and an excellent tour guide. I also played some of the best golf I'd played in months.

He didn't make any comments about my swing, but he got to grips with it quickly. On the 8th hole, Red Braes, you drive over a small cottage (a halfway house of sorts during the summer) and Philip turned to offer his advice.

'OK,' Philip said, 'you see the chimney on the cottage.'

'Aim over that?' I asked.

'No. Three tiles left of the chimney. The way you hit the ball, that's your line.'

One of two things was going to happen: I was either going to smack my drive straight into the cottage or I was going to hit it exactly where he suggested. My ball obeyed and when we walked up onto the fairway it was dead centre.

'I tried a camper van once,' Philip remarked as we played the 10th hole, with Van Morrison's beloved Coney Island beyond. 'Four of us drove down to Kerry to play in a tournament and we went on the cheap.'

My mind flickered to Rusty, supposedly a four-person camper van, which I'd long ago established to be some form of cruel joke, presumably created by the Lilliputians.

'By the time we arrived in Kerry, we booked into a B&B. We all agreed: never again.'

I didn't keep score but thanks to Philip, my self-belief soared. What is it about golf that allows you to do that . . . to walk up to a shot and just think about what you want the ball to do before executing it perfectly?

After my greatly improved golf at Ardglass, my hopes were high that I could do justice to one of the world's top five courses. It is a tribute to the reputation and beauty of Royal County Down that seeing the Mourne Mountains and then the Slieve Donard Hotel raises goosebumps before you even see the course.

I had the pleasure of playing this Shangri-La, in Newcastle,

County Down, with two good buddies, Finbarr and Mike. Finbarr had been my partner in crime already on my travels, but Mike had flown in from New York that morning.

Stepping onto the car park tarmac and then RCD's hallowed turf does things to a man, which may explain why we walked to the 1st tee and discovered we were on the wrong course. The Annesley course, or Mourne Golf Club, is inter-linked with Royal County Down and is an entertaining par sixty-six, but it wasn't what we were after.

The Starter called us over and I felt a trickle of sweat wind its way down my forehead. I am not a golfer who likes to be observed on the 1st tee, which is one of the joys of playing at 7 a.m. On this occasion it brought back unexpected memories.

When I lived in the UK many years ago, the company I worked for sponsored the British Masters at the Forest of Arden, outside Birmingham. I was given the opportunity to invite a guest to the Sponsor's Day, which took place the day after Monty won. I invited Robert from my printing supplier, partly because he was a good bloke but mostly because he played off a 4 handicap and the event was a four-ball better-ball.

On the day, I was surprised to see a Starter announcing golfers onto the tee, his voice booming through loud speakers that had been left over from the tournament. Each announcement was followed by polite applause from about thirty people who were greeting the golfers.

'Sorry I'm late, very sorry,' bleated John as he rushed towards me, pulling a set of clubs.

'Where's Robert?' I asked, looking over his shoulder.

'Oh,' said John, 'I decided that as the managing director I should come along instead.'

I didn't have the luxury of time to get annoyed or to point

out that he hadn't been invited, as the man by the Starter's hut was waving frantically at us.

'On the tee, from One2One, is Kevin Markham, playing off 13.' The voice blasted through the speakers into my ears.

John's eyes went wide. 'What . . .?' he started to ask, before I climbed the steps to the tee. I rushed the practice swing as the Starter gave me some words of encouragement, but I was so put off by the last couple of minutes that I barely noticed the people watching me. I banged my drive down the fairway.

I couldn't see John when I walked back to my bag.

'On the tee, from One2One, is Robert Scully, playing off 4.' As my guest, the timesheet listed Robert as One2One. I suppose that was one blessing . . . for John at least.

A man I barely recognised as the managing director of our printing company – someone who struck multi-million pound deals across the world – trudged up onto the tee box. I caught his eye and saw sheer terror festering. He teed up his ball and took a practice swing.

'Dear God,' I muttered, watching a swing straight out of a medieval sword fight. This wasn't going to be pretty. There was a general unease in the crowd behind me, and some took a cautionary step backwards.

They needn't have worried: John missed the ball entirely with his first attempt.

We all held our breath as he made a second attempt. Some couldn't watch, some couldn't look away and I realised I was in for a long, long round of golf. This time the ball bounced once off the tee box, went airborne reluctantly and then took cover in the rough.

The round took six-and-a-half hours, with John refusing to pick up his ball, even though it was a Stableford competition.

'I need the practice,' was his rationale.

'You need to go and drown your sorry ass,' muttered one of the others.

How bad was he? On one hole it took him nine shots to reach my drive; on one green he took six putts. When we wrote down his final score, the scorecard spontaneously combusted.

At Royal County Down these thoughts were far too close to the surface as I stepped up to my drive. I was a single figure golfer now, I had the honour and it was a perfect golfing day. The 1st hole is a par five and my mind should have been thinking birdie. Instead, it was thinking 'just don't miss the ball'.

I didn't miss the ball. I managed to catch enough of the white shell to knock it off the tee and move it sideways, about 12 inches. I think Finbarr ruptured something he laughed so hard. I picked up the ball, replaced it and tried again with considerably more success.

Royal County Down is a special moment in a golfer's life. Those first tingles and thrills will never be repeated. Stand on the 4th tee and be amazed by the beauty of the mountains and the steeple ahead of you; walk around the dune in front of the 9th tee, and breathe it in; relish huge tufts of grasses exploding from the bunkers' edges, reminiscent of the eyebrows of your favourite uncle. And if you feel nothing, then come off at 9 and have your pulse taken to check you're not dead.

The three of us debated Royal County Down in great depth after the round, choosing to ignore our golfing performance and my opening drive for obvious reasons. Jack Nicklaus is not a fan of the course because of the number of blind shots, but we didn't feel that way. Sometimes the pure joy of playing a course like this makes such concerns redundant. RCD has been a golfing entity since 1889, and to take away those blind shots would be to remove much of the course's charm and soul. You have to play it as it comes and roll with the punches.

As Finbarr and Mike made tracks in a different direction, I followed the road west to Kilkeel and Warrenpoint. From there I steered north to begin a second loop that would turn Northern Ireland's golf courses into a figure of eight on my map.

By the time I reached Loughgall Golf Club, fifteen minutes' drive north of Armagh town, the dark swarm of mosquitoes had been following me for a couple of days. In Ireland, there aren't many bugs to worry about: partly because they're confined to gnats, mosquitoes, wasps and horse flies; and partly because they're too busy chasing me. I am one of those people whom everyone loves to have at a barbeque, because once I arrive the insects are interested in no one else. Sharks can smell blood from a mile away; bugs can smell me from ten. I have sweet blood. There have been times when I felt I should simply stick a drip in my arm and put an 'all-you-can-eat-buffet' sign above my head. When I go to play golf, I don't spray on insect repellent, I take a bath in it.

After I parked at the club, which includes football pitches and a camping site, I watched the mossies set up tents, light campfires and sing 'Kumbaya' as night descended.

There were other camper vans alongside me. I peered out the window at two men sitting in fold-up chairs, smacking liberally at their necks and arms, and sighed in resignation. They'd be safe now that I'd arrived.

Lying in bed that night, just as I turned off the light, I heard the one sound that terrifies more than any other: the distant whine of a mosquito. I almost sat bolt upright, but this time my brain engaged before my head collided with the ceiling.

Having moaned for much of the trip that Rusty was too small, I discovered that it was enormous and that the buzzing mosquito liked to play Grandma's Footsteps. I turned on the light, jumped down and stood poised in the middle of the camper. Nothing. I moved back to the bed and switched off the light. The whining started. I turned the light on. The whining stopped. Off, on, off, on and every time the whining got closer until I finally spotted her. *Golf Monthly* magazine is useful for many things, and killing mosquitoes can now be added to the list. It was scant consolation because I lay awake for the rest of the night, flinching at the slightest sound.

I sneaked out for an early morning round, only to find a note pinned to the door on my return. The words 'We know where you live' were scrawled in tiny letters. When I looked more closely, the scrawl was in blood. Evidently, my fellow camper van travellers had not been as lucky as I had thought.

A mosquito bite is an infuriating thing and I endured several. The male mosquito does not bite and flies silently. At least the female has the decency to give you fair warning, although how one found itself in the vicinity of my crotch remains a mystery. It was a nasty bite, too, one that required a lot of itching, which is never a good thing when you excuse yourself to the bushes and then discover, mid-itch, that you're standing by the 10th tee on Ladies' Day. I think I scarred the women of Moyola Park Golf Club for life.

After leaving the languid landscapes of County Armagh, I had a much safer visit to Killymoon in County Tyrone. The club is a few hundred metres from Cookstown town and I was happily settled into the bar, watching light sparkle off another glitterball. This was the third clubhouse on this trip, which had been adorned with such a 1980s' throwback. I couldn't figure out if Northern Ireland was a couple of decades behind everybody else, or whether courses down south were missing a trick.

Golf clubs forever promote themselves as a 'hidden gem' or 'the jewel in the crown'. Perhaps some clubs this side of the Border should start adding 'glitterball of the north' to that list of clichés.

The A29 took me farther north towards the Sperrin Mountains, a stretch of rumpled peaks renowned for their terrible winter weather. I had been rain-free for many days, the skies much exhausted after the deluge of August. In some of the clubs I played they were making repeated attempts to hold their Captain's Day after total washouts. I sympathised. Dunmurry Golf Club outside Belfast had required four attempts.

The August floods had caused damage unlike anything I'd seen before on a golf course and, over the coming weeks, I would discover its true scale. But first came the world famous links courses of counties Derry and Antrim.

My first stop was Castlerock, the somewhat unloved sister of a triumvirate that includes Portstewart and Royal Portrush. As the crow flies, this is a 5-mile, Atlantic Ocean coastline of golf. It embraces six 18-hole courses.

'What was the *craic* like?'

It was a question fired at me time and again. And time and again I had to say that I didn't always know because during the winter, and often during spring and autumn, clubhouses closed at 6 p.m.

In terms of the *craic*, my visit to Castlerock rates as one of the best. Not only did I stagger out of the clubhouse at close to midnight, I staggered out again at 2 p.m. the following day.

It was the club's President's Day and the afternoon had

turned miserable, the wind hurrying in, dragging a reluctant rain in its wake. In the face of such angst, several golfers had returned to the clubhouse to drown their sorrows. Sitting in the bar, my laptop out, there was that volume which comes only from the enjoyably inebriated.

'What you doing?' A bleary-eyed man stared at me and then scooted unsteadily around behind my chair to investigate. He leaned forward and was so close I could smell how long before his Guinness had been pulled.

'I'm writing a book on the golf courses of Ireland,' I explained, finding myself leaning at a precarious angle.

'Mr President,' he roared, not thinking to move his mouth away from my ear. 'I have a golf book here writing a man.'

The President pottered over, shook my hand and welcomed me. 'We're just getting started.' He was fresh from his fiftieth wedding anniversary, so I wasn't sure to whom the 'we' referred. After all, what better way to celebrate fifty years of marriage than with a day at the golf club.

And then Big Merv arrived. He settled down in the chair opposite and we began chatting. A mine of information was Merv. Not, he happily admitted, a proper golfer, which was amusing since two of his brothers-in-law were the professionals at Bundoran and Donegal. And then Paul arrived, yet another brother-in-law.

'Some years back,' Paul started, as we discussed Castlerock's pedigree, 'Merv, Dad and myself were caddying for a bunch of Americans. It was some four-ball, too. Michael Douglas, Dan Marino, the guy who owns the Miami Dolphins and his son. When word got around a crowd of interested locals descended on the course and we were surrounded. On one of the tee boxes a thirteen-year-old we knew walked up to Dan Marino and asks who he is and what he does.

'I'm a footballer,' Marino said.

'Yeah?' countered the boy, 'you any good?'

'I was OK,' Marino replied. 'Actually, I was the best there's ever been.'

Dan Marino was the 6-foot-4-inch quarterback for the Miami Dolphins for seventeen years in the 1980s and 1990s. In essence, he was the Colin Montgomerie of American football and was regarded as a giant of the game but one who was never able to bring home the big prize. He broke more records than you can shake a stick at, so being asked who he was must have been an interesting change.

We moved to the bar as the evening wore on, pulled out stools and discussed golf, rugby, politics, and Castlerock history. We also discussed Nicola, the pretty young lass behind the bar.

'My son's mad about her,' Merv said. Nicola blushed and then beamed a smile at us. 'Trouble is,' Merv continued, 'he's in America and she's here.'

Nicola carried on beaming for most of the night as she was drawn into the conversation; with a smile like that I don't recommend Merv's son stay away too long.

I remembered little else from that night, apart from the bar shutters being pulled down and me shaking off offers to go on somewhere else. I was due on the tee at 7.30 a.m. and I didn't believe in missing my tee time, not on a weekend.

By 7.15 a.m. there was a heaving throng around the clubhouse and 1st tee. I was invited to play with Tommy, Cedric and Jimmy. Tommy was the oldest and in a buggy, minding his two plastic hips as he was off on a two-week holiday to Puerto Rico the next morning. What other sport would allow you the freedom to play with two plastic hips?

First there was Moira at Youghal, and now Tommy. And he was a bundle of energy.

Golf is a game that can be played at two (if your name's Tiger Woods) or 102. Don't believe me? In 2007, Elsie McLean was playing golf in California when she aced a 100-yard par three . . . at 102 years of age. Only swimming can possibly hope to compete with the longevity of golfers, which explains why, in terms of numbers, they're officially the two most popular sports in the world.

I didn't ask Tommy's age, but his number-crunching was impressive as he tied us in to a competitive four-ball match for most of the money in my wallet. I partnered Tommy and we were one down after eight – our birdie on the par five 5th being trumped by Jimmy's eagle – then two down after eleven when Cedric rolled in a 30-footer for birdie. We were playing in sunshine, but I wasn't happy at Cedric and Jimmy's blatant banditry.

'Try a drop of this,' Tommy instructed on the 12th tee, handing me a small bottle. No doubt he was hoping the potion might inspire us to catch the boys.

My alcohol level had barely abated since the previous night, but it would have been rude to refuse. 'What is it?' I asked, before taking a slug of the entertainingly reddish liquid.

By way of an answer, someone I didn't see hit me in the back of the head with a 3 iron, and then sucker punched me in the gut for good measure. My eyes spun, my throat burned and my lungs turned to dust.

'Bishop Daly's Special Brew,' laughed Tommy, taking a swig. 'Good, isn't it?' He handed it back to me.

'Good' wouldn't have been my description. It was exquisite.

After two sips, I could barely stand. After three, I had half a dozen balls to choose from during my downswing. Even so, I played the last eight holes in level par, evidently so carefree that my swing was as relaxed and easy as it has ever been. It was to no avail as we lost a further hole. Three down overall and Tommy had forty-two points on his card. We were all rather impressed with ourselves as we walked off the 18th green.

Castlerock is a fine links, constantly changing pace and style to make you work the whole way around. With its crumpled dunes and the blue whale buried in the middle of the 12th fairway, you'll be tossed about in true links style.

'Come on, Tommy, let's have the ingredients of that elixir of yours?' I asked as we sat in the bar, surrounded by Castlerock's early morning golfers.

Tommy was reluctant to tell me, but I later discovered that the three core ingredients are poitín, Bombay Gin and brandy balls. Throw in some secret ingredients and you have a drink that is powerful enough to sink even John Daly in his prime.

The lads all left for their day's obligations and I sat in the bar in no fit state to go anywhere. As if on cue, after a beautifully sunny morning, it promptly began to rain. I sighed and indicated to the barman that it was time for another pint.

To reach Portstewart from Castlerock you take two long sides of a triangle around the Bann estuary, with Coleraine on the southern tip. I was offered a university place here in 1986, but I had not been back since my interviews. It is a pretty and affluent town with a population of 25,000, and the high property prices are due, in part, to the championship golf courses nearby and the beauty of the surrounding landscape.

I got to enjoy both when I played Portstewart's Strand

course, only a few miles to the north of Coleraine. Portstewart has two other 18-hole courses but it is the Strand that people come to play. I spent the night on the other side of town, parked in the Old Course car park. It's a small holiday course and the place was deserted, so I took an easy stroll along the coast road and ended up on the sea front in no more than five minutes. It's that small a town. The bars were buzzing and despite it being close to 10 p.m. you'd have thought it was midday. I was sidestepping animated groups of young people and paying more attention to what these people held in their hands than where I was going.

'Mmmm, Snickers,' I heard a woman gasp.

'Honeycomb,' countered another.

'This strawberry is so sweet,' said a third.

I had landed in the town of ice cream and yet my hands and mouth were empty. I was figuring out who I could mug when I spotted the bright neon lights of Morelli's. The style of the place is 1950s' American diner, but the choice of ice cream is designed for today's 'must have' generation: whatever you want, Morelli's pretty much has it. This is a family business that opened on the Portstewart Promenade in 1911. It has won awards but, more importantly, it has won the hearts and minds of tourists and locals alike.

I walked in, calmly tossing women and children aside, and asked for a table. The place was packed, but I guess the girl noted the look on my face and made space for me. Morelli's serves far more than ice cream, but my eyes ignored all other items on the menu as they scrolled down to Ice Cream Sundaes. This was my utopia.

According to the menu, 'Morelli's Madness' is a 'huge monster of a sundae with no fewer than seven scoops of ice cream and a little bit of pretty much everything else!!!' Three exclamation marks drove the point home. The menu also claimed that this sundae was 'ideal for sharing'. I don't think so . . . with three exclamation marks!!! Each one of those scoops had my name on it.

I ordered and sat back to enjoy the atmosphere, watching young and old enjoy themselves in this ice cream den of depravity. Once my sundae arrived, I tucked in, performing a tribute to *When Harry Met Sally* that caused several people to order the same.

Royal Portrush is 5 miles along the road. In golfing terms it ratchets things up a gear because it is the only golf course on the island to have hosted the Open Championship (1951). Maybe it will host the Open again; and maybe it won't.

I finished up in the main clubhouse, with its enormous red-tiled roof, checking out Rory McIlroy's record-breaking card on the clubhouse wall. There had been a copy at Holywood. Many of the famous courses have walls adorned with photographs of the world's top golfers. At Royal County Down there's a picture of Tiger taking a divot the size of a small country, at Ballybunion it's Tom Watson, at Mount Juliet it's Ernie Els, at Druid's Glen it's Monty . . . and at The K Club it's Michael Smurfit. Go figure.

Most clubs have shrines to international golfers and the golfers who are at the heart and soul of the club itself. Time spent wandering the corridors is a recommended part of any golf experience.

I headed east on the A2, along the Antrim coastline. It is an easy route to navigate as I followed the signposts for Bushmills. This is a village that has the enviable reputation of being home to the oldest distillery in the world. Old

Bushmills Distillery was founded in 1608 and still produces some of the world's most popular whiskeys. That's whiskey with an 'e'.

I took a detour and picked up a bottle of the good stuff for my dad, although I wasn't convinced he would ever get it.

A few miles along the road is the Giant's Causeway, the island's most popular tourist attraction, with its interlocking polygonal columns of layered basalt. It is the only World Heritage Site in Northern Ireland, attracting some 300,000 visitors a year, and it is remarkable to behold. You could start playing a game of hopscotch with your kids at one end, and be a great-granddad by the time you reach the other.

The Causeway Coastal Route continues towards Ballycastle Golf Club, but not before there's one more thrill: Carrick-a-Rede Rope Bridge. It's exactly what it says it is: a bridge made of rope. Sure sure, it's only 20 metres across, but there's a 23-metre drop into a cauldron of rocks and ocean as you inch your way from the mainland to the island of Carrick. It used to be used by fishermen; today it is popular with tourists up for a nerve-wracking experience. I joined them, struggled across, staggered back and opened Dad's whiskey.

Ballycastle, Cairndhu and Whitehead golf courses are along this Causeway Coastal Route, all offering high headlands that promise spectacular views over the sea to Scotland. From Ballycastle's 9th the Mull of Kintyre is clearly visible. It is so close that avid golfers can take a speed dinghy across the North Channel to play the two Machrahanish courses. From Cairndhu and Whitehead, farther to the south, the dome-shaped rocky outcrop that is Ailsa Craig resembles the curling stones it is famous for.

I stumbled upon roadworks in Ballymena, directly south of Ballycastle. It was an easy hour's drive, skirting the Glens of Antrim to the east, and yet I arrived at the roadworks in a rush. Organisation of roadworks in Ireland is – how shall I put this diplomatically? – shambolic, and here was no different. You rarely know they're coming until you're on top of them and one paltry cone does not qualify as fair warning when there's a trench in the road as wide as the River Shannon.

The road to Galgorm Castle Golf Club was blocked off. I started to lose my composure. I banged the steering wheel. A man walking his dog noticed my frustration, or rather he heard my roars of anger, and he calmly gave me directions that took me halfway around the town of Ballymena. For once I listened and followed his instructions. Even so, my tee time was long gone by the time I arrived. I stomped across the car park, happy to let this particular black cloud dictate my mood only for Gary Henry, the general manager, to slot me in with no trouble at all.

Standing on the 1st tee I was angry and frustrated. It was not a good way to start. I was tense, forgot my warm-up ritual and swatted at the ball without giving it the respect it deserved. Even so, it found the fairway. Holes one and two slipped quickly by and I found myself on the 3rd tee behind a four-ball of a man with three young boys. While I waited I looked at the surroundings and noticed large quantities of detritus in the trees beside the river. Shopping bags, crisp packets, even beer cans were caught up in the branches, easily at chest height. What a bizarre place to throw your rubbish, I thought, as I hit my drive.

The four-ball let me through on the 4th, where the five of us drove towards the river.

'Are you visiting?' Desmond enquired after introducing himself and the three boys. He was a club member and he was interested in my thoughts on the condition of the course.

'Yes,' I replied. I thought the course looked in great nick, apart from the rubbish, and I told him so.

He nodded to himself. 'Would you believe that only two weeks ago three of our holes were under water following the floods? The hole you've just played is one of them, and you'd have been up to your waist where you're standing now.'

I had seen photos on the walls of Ballyclare Golf Club, 15 miles away, that showed the devastation caused by the floods. Their bunkers were crushed and empty, the paths washed away and greens left drowned in mud, but apart from the rubbish in the trees, you'd never have known Galgorm Castle had been submerged at all.

We'd reached our drives and I hit my second to a few feet from the flag. 'Nice shot.' Desmond leaned against his trolley and looked around him. 'We opened the course a few days later and it's as good as it ever was.'

'Ballyclare must have been hit worse than you. I saw photos of the after-effects,' I said. 'They were hammered.'

'We both were. I have some photographs if you'd like to see them. I took them from the bridge behind the 3rd tee . . . during the flooding.'

'During? What, you came by boat, did you?'

He laughed and gave me a big smile. 'Something like that.'

I gave him my card and he promised to email some shots as he waved me on my way. They waved again after I sank my birdie putt and I hurried on to the 5th tee.

The bridge on the way to the green held more evidence of the scale of the flooding. This was where the River Main looped, ox-bow like, around the 4th green and the 5th and 15th tee boxes, on its way to meet the River Braid farther down the course. By the time I returned to the same spot an hour or so later, to play the 15th, I was three under par. Galgorm Castle is a wonderfully lazy, elegant parkland where you drift through the trees and over water. Evidently, it is also extremely easy.

Before I started this adventure, I had set myself two goals: to record a hole in one and to play at least one round in level par. The former comes down to luck, but the latter was always within my control. Several times I had been standing on the 18th tee, either level or one over, only to blow my chances. I tried relaxing, I tried playing aggressively, but whatever I did it didn't work. What is worse, perhaps, is knowing that you're going to fall to pieces because that's what has happened every other time. The body may be willing, but the mind has different ideas and turns my swing to jelly and my hands to lead.

I had yet to achieve either ambition and I had only a handful of courses to go so, as I walked off the 15th green with a par, I calculated that a dropped shot on each of the final three holes would still leave me level par.

On the 18th, a par five, I stood on the tee waiting for a four-ball to get out of range.

'Come on, mate,' I muttered to myself, 'a triple bogey, that's all you need for glory.' You simply can't beat the power of negative positivity.

It's a worrying sign when you're urging yourself to a triple; it's even more worrying when you're pacing the tee box talking to yourself. All I required was an eight and there wasn't a drop of water in sight. No, I didn't see a Van de Velde moment in my future.

By the time I reached the green some time later I felt sick. Where was Bishop Brady's Special Brew when I needed it? I had waited on each shot for the group in front to clear and now it was me, the ball and a two-foot putt.

A few minutes later I was checking my card in the camper van when the phone rang. It was one of my clients. We talked about the brochure I was writing for him.

'You sound out of breath. Are you OK?' Barry asked.

'Yes, fine. I'm just off the golf course and I went around in four under par.'

'Oh, I see. Is that good?' He paused. 'When do you think you can have that copy for me?'

I bumped into Frank Ainsworth as I played Hilton Templepatrick the following day. He was busy around the greens and stood back to let me play.

'Yep, our 12th was a good five feet underwater. Opened for play two days later,' he replied to my question about flooding.

'Is that why the greens look so dark?' They were superb putting surfaces but there were odd patches splashed across them.

'Not at all. We dressed them in ferrous sulphate.'

Chemistry was never my strong suit at school. I once had to write out the Chemical table ten times for detention. Didn't do much good though. All I remember is that Fe is iron, K is Kryptonite and O_2 is a mobile phone company.

'Have you played Edenmore or Foyle or Gracehill?' Frank asked.

'All three.'

'What did you think?'

I thought long and hard about my answer. For much of my life I have spent many an occasion removing my foot from my mouth, and I have learned that direct questions usually have ulterior motives.

'I really liked Gracehill. I played it last week and found the solitude charming. Why do you ask?'

'I designed them.'

Probably just as well I hadn't been honest about Foyle or Edenmore.

I had been privileged enough to see Bunclody and Farnham Estate in the throes of coming into this world, and I saw Concra Wood before anyone had played it, but I had never had a conversation with a bona fide course architect, and I told him so.

He smiled at the flattery. 'Actually, I was asked to pitch for the job of designing Concra Wood. Next thing I knew, Christy O'Connor Senior and Junior had been chosen. It's a beautiful piece of land, though, and I'd love to have worked on it.'

After my initial concerns about Northern Ireland, I had encountered no problems or confrontations of any kind, other than at Kirkistown Castle. That all changed at Massereene Golf Club outside Antrim town. It was ironic since it was the last golf club I had to play. It started well, too, with a busy evening in the clubhouse, chatting to members who were excited about the President's Prize the following day. It was midnight when the trouble started. A bang on the camper van door woke me.

'*Yushkenbysersh!*' the man at the door exploded at me. He was young, thin and loud. He was also very drunk.

I hadn't struggled with any Northern Ireland accents up to that point, but, combined with his alcohol-induced speech impediment, the man was indecipherable.

He was not alone. He was being propped up like a ventriloquist's dummy by another lad who looked far too sober by comparison. He smiled weakly as I turned to him. 'What did he say?'

I swear his lips didn't move as the words were repeated: '*Yushkenbysersh!*'

When I contacted Massereene, Gary, the general manager, asked if I could tee off at 6 a.m., and if I could park near the clubhouse in the Lady Captain's parking space. He said he'd pass the word around.

Only, the word hadn't reached a few members . . . a few very drunk members who decided at midnight that my camper van was a problem. After the door was almost banged off its hinges, I was confronted by the only ventriloquist act in golf.

The situation wasn't helped when one of my shoes decided to fall out of the camper. It bounced down the steps and landed in front of them. The drunk's head dropped forward to have a look at the offending item. It was a pose reminiscent of a Labrador staring at food on the floor that it has been instructed not to eat. Nose down, ears flapping forward, tail in a slow perplexed wag. Fortunately the man didn't appear to be drooling.

We all pondered the shoe for a moment.

Was I supposed to get out to retrieve the shoe and give up the high ground? Was he physically able to bend that far without falling head first into the camper van? The silent one couldn't do anything since his arms were already being used to hold the other guy upright.

I was still trying to decipher his earlier words. I factored in the accent until I eventually realised he'd said 'You can't be serious.'

'Serious about what?' I replied.

He dragged his eyes away from the shoe and stared off into the distance trying to gauge where the voice had come from. His sidekick hoisted him up so that he was facing me, but the eyes continued to drift in a number of different directions.

He returned to planet earth. 'Oh, yeah, you can't park

here.' There was no aggression in the statement but he and his group of friends nearby had decided that I wasn't staying.

'It's fine. I'm playing the course tomorrow and Gary told me to park here.' I replied, before explaining that it had all been cleared with the club. Their initial incomprehension turned to some form of understanding. They nodded knowledgeably – well, they nodded – and then my drunken friend tried to pick up the shoe. After several flailing attempts he made contact and handed me the shoe.

'Gudgenite,' he muttered as he was steered away, back to his friends.

'Goodnight,' I returned. Somehow I knew we weren't through.

I closed the door and listened, still holding the shoe. Someone else in the group started giving out that just because I knew the name Gary didn't mean a thing. I wondered what they thought I was doing. I wanted to point out that if I was trying to park on the sly, I wouldn't park within five feet of the clubhouse, under the security lights, in the Lady Captain's parking space. Especially when there were plenty of places that were out of sight. And if I was going to guess a name, it wouldn't have been 'Gary'. But then logic and alcohol are not exactly bosom buddies.

At 2 a.m. there was another knock on the door. I was actually grateful to see through the blinds the flashing blue lights of a police car. I slid out of bed, failing to realise that my exceedingly comfortable bed shorts had ridden up over my considerably ample stomach and were now resting somewhere slightly south of my armpits. I was an Irish Obelisk, but without the flair or the hair. Or the full length pants for that matter. By rising northwards, my shorts had left my southern extremities somewhat exposed. It was not a pretty sight as the female police officer quickly discovered.

'Hello,' the policewoman said, taking a step back – a very sensible move on her part – and averting her gaze, another very sensible move. 'We've been informed that something suspicious might be going on here.'

It was at this point I noticed the interesting positioning of my shorts. Yes, suspicious indeed. I made the necessary adjustments.

'I take it you got a call from someone saying I shouldn't park here?'

'That's about right,' she said, finally feeling safe enough to face me again.

'Could you understand a word he said?'

She frowned at that one and said it wasn't she who took the call.

I explained who I was and gave her my card. She looked at it briefly, nodding to herself.

'That's fine,' she said. 'Sorry to have troubled you.' She gave my shorts one final glance before returning to the car where her partner sat.

I was still standing there when they drove away. They weren't that interested at all, not even in my wardrobe malfunction.

Not surprisingly, I slept through my alarm and arrived on the tee late. It was still dark and I spent the first three holes fumbling my way through the tiredness of my mind and the weak morning light. By 9 a.m. I was standing on the 18th green, with Lough Neagh behind me, rolling the ball into the cup.

The golfers on the practice green must have wondered what was going on as I raised my arms skyward and let out a tired but satisfied shout. With that putt I had played every 18-hole golf course on the island.

I met Gary in the clubhouse and he was mortified when

I told him about my encounters of the previous evening. It mattered little, and it was one of those odd encounters that makes travelling so entertaining. And besides, I had finished. It was over and I was still standing.

So was Rusty. I left Massereene and began my final journey home.

Journey's End

'If I had to choose between my wife and my putter, I'd miss her.'

GARY PLAYER

I did not sink my final putt on some big glamorous course. It would have been wrong to do so. The purpose of my travels was always to find the special courses that golfers don't know about. Massereene fit the bill, with its relaxed yet distinguished air; like so many other courses, it had come as a complete surprise.

I don't deny that playing the famous courses were experiences never to be forgotten, but finding the gems was equally rewarding. The Strandhills, Rathcores, Scrabos and Portumnas of this island can hold their heads high and know that they offer superb golf experiences, if only people would go and play them and spread the word.

I had thought that ending the book with some final tale about Rusty was the way to go, but it was depressing to see it sitting in the yard for so long, assaulted by the autumn and winter weather. I barely set foot in it again in the months that followed. My friend Charlie suggested that after all the angst it had caused me we should take it to a field and hit golf balls at it. Yes, it let me down, but it had to travel 11,000 kilometres and I wasn't exactly gentle, what with my many parking mishaps. Besides, it had one final day of glory as I headed to the magnificent European Club to be interviewed for an article in *Today's Golfer* magazine. I spent the night before cleaning her from top to bottom and she shone in the sunlight as Angus took photos of the interior and exterior, before Kevin Browne and I went out on the course to play some of Pat Ruddy's masterpiece.

No, for the ending I should go back to the start, to that small course called Charleville in County Cork. It was probably the tenth course I played and as myself and playing partner Geoff approached the 18th tee he suggested we put a bet on the final hole. I agreed and drove first. His tee shot veered to the right, blocking him from the green. His second was worse, skidding off into the trees.

'What a dreadful shot,' he muttered.

Then he stopped and glanced at me with a rueful look on his face. 'Actually, that was a fantastic shot.'

I frowned. 'How so?' No golfer in the world would have been happy with that shot, but that was Geoff's point.

'There's a local farmer around here who used to play golf. One day he went into a barn where the bull was kept. The animal should have been tied up but someone hadn't done it, and when he walked in the bull gored him, throwing him up into the ceiling. He's paralysed from the neck down and will never walk again.' He shrugged and headed after his ball. 'By comparison, any shot I hit is a great shot, and I'm thankful to be playing golf at all.'

231

Epilogue

St Andrews, Pebble Beach, Valderrama, Royal Melbourne, Augusta. Whatever courses are on your bucket list remember this: nothing will ever rise to the beauty of those Irish golf courses where the landscapes tug at the heartstrings, the challenges leave you breathless and the friendliness makes you never want to leave.

I have been blessed to play Ireland's courses. There is nothing more I could ask for . . . except one final thing: when I die, I want my ashes taken to the county of Donegal, to a quiet seaside village that rests on the edge of Gweebarra Bay. And there, with a sweeping vista of Narin Strand, Inniskeel Island and the Blue Stack Mountains, I want those ashes released on the tee of Narin &  Portnoo's short par four 8th. With the sun bright and a stiff, cold northerly wind beating in from the Atlantic, I will find eternal peace. And, if the wind is willing, I will reach the green in one.